Designing a Comprehensive
Early Intervention System

Designing a Comprehensive Early Intervention System

THE CHALLENGE OF PUBLIC LAW 99-457

S. Gray Garwood
SOUTH CAROLINA CENTER FOR EXCELLENCE IN EARLY CHILDHOOD

Robert Sheehan
CLEVELAND STATE UNIVERSITY

8700 Shoal Creek Boulevard
Austin, Texas 78758

KF
4197
.G37
1989

Printed in the United States of America.

Library of Congress Cataloging-in-Publication Data

Garwood, S. Gray.
    Designing a comprehensive early intervention
system.

    Includes index.
    1. Education, Preschool – Law and legislation –
United States. 2. Handicapped children – Education –
Law and legislation – United States. 3. Special
education – Law and legislation – United States.
4. Handicapped children – Education, Preschool –
United States. 5. Special education – United States.
I. Sheehan, Robert, 1951– . II. Title.
KF4197.G37   344.73′074   89-3835
ISBN 0-89079-202-X   347.30474

8700 Shoal Creek Boulevard
Austin, Texas 78758

10 9 8 7 6 5 4 3 2 1   89 90 91 92 93 94

.222228
OCLC: 19457656
DEC 5 1990

Contents

Preface

This volume was designed to help professionals implement the portion of Public Law 99-457 calling for the establishment of statewide, comprehensive, coordinated, multidisciplinary programs of early intervention services for all handicapped infants and toddlers and their families. The transition from a law passed in 1986 to a national reality in 1991 will require considerable state and local initiative. Early intervention professionals must quickly become familiar with this legislation, identify eligible infants and toddlers and their families, analyze existing service systems and unmet needs, and design and implement a statewide system that complements and coordinates existing services without supplanting those services.

The four chapters in this volume each address a critical aspect of P.L. 99-457. Chapter 1 provides an analysis of the historical antecedents of P.L. 99-457. The linkage between P.L. 99-457 and the Education for All Handicapped Children Act (P.L. 99-142) is made clear, and the rationale for intervention with handicapped and at-risk infants and toddlers is presented. Chapter 2 presents relevant reprints of P.L. 99-457 as well as critical excerpts of the Committee Report accompanying this law. The Committee Report clarifies and amplifies congressional intent. Chapter 2 also presents the regulations proposed for P.L. 99-457 as of the writing of this text (late summer, 1988).

Chapter 3 carefully describes each mandated component of a statewide, comprehensive early intervention system. This chapter also provides a number of substantive resources available to early intervention personnel to develop each component in detail. Finally, Chapter 4 provides a detailed data collection system addressing each of the mandated components of a statewide early intervention system. Numerous instruments and data collection strategies are provided along with suggestions for data coding and analysis. Instruments suggested in Chapter 4 are also of great use in gathering data at a regional or local level.

In many ways, passage of P.L. 99-457 represents a significant challenge to the early intervention community. All states have accepted the challenge to design a statewide, comprehensive, coordinated system, building upon the often fragmented array of existing service delivery systems. The amount of interagency planning that must be accomplished in such an effort is enormous. Public Law 99-457 is quite explicit, though, in its emphasis that infants and toddlers must be served while interagency linkages are being negotiated. By 1991, the often bewildering array of needs and service options facing the families of handicapped infants and toddlers must be fit within a coherent, comprehensive, coordinated system. P.L. 99-457 represents a strong national commitment to the belief that life can be made more manageable and hopeful for very young children who are at risk in our society. This volume represents an effort to help realize that goal.

Acknowledgments

Several of our colleagues provided significant assistance in the development of this volume. We gratefully acknowledge the assistance of Dr. Sam Odom who assisted in the design of early drafts of many of the data collection instruments found in Chapter 4. We also note, with thanks, the funding provided to Dr. Sheehan and Dr. Odom by the Indiana Department of Mental Health and Project First Steps to develop early drafts of these data collection tools. In particular, the advice of Ms. Doree Bedwell and Ms. Mary Short is appreciated. The administration and staff at our respective organizations — Winthrop College, Center for Excellence; and Cleveland State University, College of Education — are to be thanked for their support and assistance in the development of this volume. Our greatest acknowledgment is made to the numerous early intervention personnel throughout the country who have begun the planning and development process in designing comprehensive statewide early intervention systems. We hope this volume helps them to carry on their tasks.

1

The History Behind
Enactment of P.L. 99-457

The passage of Public Law 99-457 has brought the field of education for handicapped infants and young children to a critical juncture. (Burke, McLaughlin, & Valdivieso, 1988, p. 73)

With P.L. 99-457 and related state policy developments, ECSE can achieve the fundamental programmatic framework from which to operate. (Smith & Strain, 1988, p. 37)

The provisions and implementation of P.L. 94-142 have had a major impact on the way programs for children with handicaps have been conducted at both the local and state levels. P.L. 99-457 is even more dramatic in its provisions and in what it expects to be changed or added as a part of service delivery, especially for children with handicaps from birth through age 2. (Harbin, 1988, p. 24)

The passage of Public Law 99-457 draws special education into a new era. (Odom, Yoder, & Hill, 1988, p. 11)

On October 8, 1986, P.L. 99-457 became law. It provides significantly enhanced financial incentives to states to help them provide early intervention services for *all* eligible preschoolers, and it funds state planning and development initiatives designed to create a "statewide, comprehensive, coordinated, multidisciplinary, interagency program of early intervention services for all handicapped infants and toddlers and their families" (House Report 99-860). All 50 states, the District of Columbia, Puerto Rico, and the territories have agreed to participate in developing such a system, and the purpose of this book is to help those involved at the state and local level with developing

1

and implementing this early intervention system for infants and toddlers and their families.

Who is this book for? The focus of this book is on the development of early intervention services for *infants and toddlers*, from birth through age 2, inclusive, and their families. While P.L. 99-457 also addresses the need to provide early intervention services to preschoolers, this portion of the law will receive only minimal attention in this text. Instead, we will concentrate our attention on what is termed *Part H* of the law (see Table 1.1). Part H establishes the provisions in federal law that describe the necessary components of a state's early intervention system for infants and toddlers and their families.

Unlike P.L. 94-142, which deals specifically with *special education* as the primary intervention activity, P.L. 99-457 deals with *early intervention*, which is broader than special education. While early intervention will likely include special education, it also can focus on nonspecial education activities that are deemed appropriate early intervention activities. Early intervention services are broadly defined in the new law and can include a variety of services, taken singly or in combination, depending on the needs of the eligible infant and that infant's family. Early intervention services include family training, counseling, speech pathology and audiology, occupational therapy, physical therapy, psychological services, limited medical and health services, screening and assessment services, and special instruction.

Who will administer this new law in the state? While P.L. 94-142 is always administered by state education departments, the same is not true of P.L. 99-457. It can be administered by *any* agency within a state that the governor of that state designates. Only 18 states have designated their Departments of Education as the lead agency; the remainder of the states have designated state agencies such as Health, Mental Health, Mental Retardation, Developmental Disabilities, Human Services, Human Resources, and Welfare. Maryland has designated the Governor's Office of Children and Youth as the lead agency, and the governors of Maine, Rhode Island, and Texas have given the authority to develop and implement the early intervention system to their states' Interagency Coordination Committees (Campbell, Bellamy, & Bishop, 1988; Garwood, Fewell, & Neisworth, 1988). A complete list of the state agencies and their contact persons is included in Appendix 1.

As a result of this administrative structure, persons who will be developing and implementing early intervention services for infants and toddlers and their families will represent an important new mix of professionals from a variety of disciplines. Many of these professionals will have knowledge of P.L. 94-142 and other important education laws that affect early intervention. Still others who will be working to implement this new system will be much less familiar with education law and more familiar with health law or social security legislation. We believe that this book will be useful to professionals

TABLE 1.1
Components of the Education of the Handicapped Act

Part A: General Provisions
Includes congressional findings, statement of purpose, authority for the Office of Special Education Programs within the Department of Education, definitions used in the act, authority for grants for removal of architectural barriers, authority to restrict preschool funds if a state does not serve preschoolers after fiscal year 1990 (or 1991 if a waiver has been triggered), requirements for prescribing regulations, and other matters.

Part B: Assistance for Education of All Handicapped Children (P.L. 94-142)
Provides authority for federal assistance with states' excess costs, criteria for eligibility, state planning, application and administrative guidelines, due process and judicial review procedures, program evaluation requirements, and the preschool grant program. The authority for this part is permanent unless altered by Congress. Parts C through F (described below) must be periodically reauthorized.

Part C: Centers and Services to Meet Special Needs of the Handicapped
Includes authority for regional resource and federal centers, services for deaf-blind children and youth, early education for handicapped children, programs for the severely handicapped, postsecondary education programs, secondary education and transitional services for handicapped youth, and authorization of appropriations for these programs.

Part D: Training Personnel for the Education of the Handicapped
Provides authority for grants to states and to institutions of higher education to provide preservice and inservice training of special education and related services personnel; includes authority to nonprofit agencies for training of parents as well as authority to establish clearinghouses, and authorization of these activities.

Part E: Research in the Education of the Handicapped
Authorizes funding of research and demonstration projects to improve the provision of special education and related services.

Part F: Instructional Media for the Handicapped
Provides authority to fund and operate the captioned films and educational media loan service program for handicapped persons.

Part G: Technology, Educational Media, and Materials for the Handicapped
Establishes authority and funding levels for grants to advance the use of new technology, media, and materials in the education of handicapped persons.

Part H: Handicapped Infants and Toddlers
Creates and authorizes funding for a program of federal assistance to the states to help them establish a comprehensive, coordinated, multidisciplinary, interagency program of early intervention services for handicapped infants and toddlers and their families.

in all these various state and local agencies as they work together to create their state's early intervention system.

In addition, we are hopeful that professionals in private agencies or non-profit agencies concerned with early intervention, advocates for young children with disabilities and their families, and parents will find the material in this book useful as they work with their state to develop a comprehensive early intervention system. Finally, as the quotes cited at the beginning of this chapter indicate, this new law should have a significant impact on the delivery of early intervention services to infants and toddlers with handicaps and their families. This book is designed to ensure that this impact is beneficial.

The following sections in this chapter provide background information regarding P.L. 99-457. Public Law 94-142 (the Education for All Handicapped Children Act) is described and related to P.L. 99-457, and the rationale for intervention with handicapped and at-risk infants and toddlers is presented.

Public Law 94-142

To many professionals and parents, P.L. 94-142 has been the pivotal law for children with special needs. Despite the importance of P.L. 94-142, it is certainly not the first piece of federal legislation providing assistance to children with disabilities. The Handicapped Children's Early Education Assistance Act, which established the HCEEP program, went into effect in 1968. Head Start, established in 1965, is administered by the Department of Health and Human Services and offers educational services to preschoolers. Since 1974, Head Start has been required to serve preschoolers with handicaps as well. Many of the national laws affecting children with handicaps are summarized in Table 1.2.

Public Law 94-142 came into being because it became apparent to parents, advocates, and policymakers during the early 1970s that federal and state efforts to meet the needs of children with handicaps were inadequate. In 1975, despite nearly 20 years of federal support to special education, approximately 2 million children with handicaps were still being denied access to a free public education (Garwood, 1983a). In addition, many of the children who were receiving some special education services were not receiving appropriate services, and many were placed in inappropriate educational settings (Abeson & Zettel, 1977).

In the late 1960s and the early 1970s, a series of legal decisions established precedents dealing with assessment of children with handicaps, the right of these children to a free public education regardless of the severity of their disability, and their right to be educated in an educational environment that was least restrictive. In addition, the parents of such children had

TABLE 1.2
Significant Federal Legislation Affecting Children with Handicaps

P.L. 83-531 (1957)	Provided initial research support for study of handicapping conditions.
P.L. 85-926 (1958)	Authorized grants to institutions of higher education to train special education leadership personnel and grants to train teachers to work with mentally retarded students.
P.L. 88-164 (1963)	Established authority for development of mental retardation facilities; expanded categories of handicapped children to include mentally retarded, hard-of-hearing, deaf, speech-impaired, visually impaired, seriously emotionally disturbed, crippled, or other health-impaired children needing special education.
P.L. 89-313 (1965)	Provided assistance to state-operated institutional programs for handicapped children.
P.L. 89-750 (1966)	Authorized funds to initiate, improve, and expand programs for the handicapped; created the Bureau of the Handicapped (now the Office of Special Education Programs) and established the National Advisory Committee on Handicapped Children (now defunct).
P.L. 90-170 (1967)	Authorized programs in physical education and recreation, and the training of leadership personnel, supervisors, and researchers.
P.L. 90-538 (1968)	Inaugurated the Handicapped Children's Early Education Program (HCEEP).
P.L. 90-576 (1968)	Authorized agencies other than institutions of higher education or states to apply for training grants.
P.L. 91-230 (1970)	Authorized funds to include learning disabled children in the categorical system of special education; reinforced federal government's role in educating children with handicaps.
P.L. 91-517 (1970)	Authorized state allotments to plan services for the developmentally disabled and provided funds for construction of facilities for persons with developmental disabilities; established funding for university affiliated programs.
P.L. 93-644 (1974)	Amended Head Start legislation to require that at least 10% of total Head Start enrollment in each state be available for handicapped children and required that services be provided to meet their special needs.
P.L. 94-103 (1975)	Established the Developmental Disabilities Assistance and Bill of Rights Act; included a requirement for creation of a Protection and Advocacy system to protect the rights of the developmentally disabled.

Table 1.2 (Continued)

P.L. 94-142 (1975)	Incorporated previous benefits from judicial and legislative actions into national policy regarding the education of all handicapped children.
P.L. 98-199 (1983)	Authorized funds to states to assist in planning, developing, and implementing a comprehensive early intervention delivery system to children with handicaps from birth to age 5.
P.L. 99-457 (1986)	Authorized funds to states to establish a comprehensive, coordinated, multidisciplinary, early intervention system for infants and toddlers and their families, from birth to age 3; increased funding for states to serve all 3- to 5-year-old children with handicaps. Requires all states to serve all eligible preschoolers by 1990 (or 1991 with a 1-year waiver) or lose some federal funding.

a right to due process procedures before their children's educational status could be altered in any way. In 1975, these precedents were incorporated into national policy regarding the education of the handicapped. Public Law 94-142 was signed into law in November 1975 for the purpose of assuring that "all handicapped children have available to them . . . a free appropriate public education emphasizing special education and related services designed to meet their unique needs" (Education of the Handicapped Act, 20 U.S.C. 1401).

Numbers of Children and Youths Served

Under P.L. 94-142, also known as EHA-Part B because P.L. 94-142 became Part B of the Education of the Handicapped Act (EHA), states are required to serve all eligible children and youths between the ages of 6 and 17 (see Table 1.1). They do this by providing *special education and related services* designed to promote each child's unique developmental needs.

In school year 1985–86, the states were providing special education and related services to 3.7 million eligible children and youths between the ages of 6 and 17. Every year since school year 1978–79, the percent increase in total number served, in relation to the number served the previous year, has declined. At the same time, the total number served continues to grow but at a decelerating rate. This pattern indicates that most of the eligible children and youths between the ages of 6 and 17 are now receiving services (USDOE, 1987). Thus, for this age group, EHA-Part B has been of great help in securing for these children and youths a free and appropriate education. This success was a lesson that was not lost on Congress when it decided to face the problem of enhancing the delivery of early intervention services to infants, toddlers, and preschoolers and their families.

Under Part B of the EHA, states may provide services to eligible preschoolers between the ages of 3 and 6 if they have no law prohibiting the provision of such services. If they do provide services to preschoolers, states can receive federal monies for these children. In 1986, that amount was about $282 per child (USDOE, 1987). In addition, the federal government made incentive funds available to states to encourage them to serve preschoolers. The maximum amount that could be made available was $300 per child, but typically that amount was never reached; in fact, in 1986, states that did serve preschool children with handicaps received only about $110 per child from Preschool Incentive Grant funds (USDOE, 1987). And as Table 1.3 illustrates, preschool incentive funding, although it started out at about the same level as funding for school-aged children, did not grow nearly as rapidly as did the funding for older children. Consequently it is not surprising that states were slower to provide services to preschoolers than to older children with handicaps.

Contrast the numbers of older children receiving services with the figures for children between the ages of 3 and 6. According to the Department of Education's Ninth Annual Report, the number of children in this age range receiving services was 260,931 for 1985–86, an increase of only about 1,400 preschoolers over the previous year (USDOE, 1987). And, as Table 1.4 shows, there was great variation among the states with respect to the ages covered in the provision of services to preschoolers in 1985.

TABLE 1.3
Preschool Funding and Number of Preschoolers Served under EHA,
Compared to Total EHA Per Child Allocations, 1977–1986

Fiscal Year	Child Count	Preschool Per Child Share	EHA Per Child Share
1977	197,000	$ 63	$ 72
1978	201,000	75	159
1979	215,000	81	217
1980	232,000	108	230
1981	237,000	105	222
1982	228,000	105	233
1983	242,000	103	251
1984	253,000	104	261
1985	259,000	112	276
1986	261,008	110	282

Source: Ninth Annual Report, USDOE, 1987.

TABLE 1.4
Minimum Ages for Providing Some Level of Preschool Special Education and Related Services, by 41 States and the District of Columbia, 1985

Age	States
At birth: (N = 7)	Iowa, Maryland, Michigan, Nebraska, New Jersey, Oregon, South Dakota
Age 2:	Virginia
Age 3: (N = 14)	Alaska, California, Connecticut, District of Columbia, Hawaii, Illinois, Louisiana, Massachusetts, New Hampshire, North Dakota, Rhode Island, Texas, Washington, Wisconsin
Age 4: (N = 4)	Delaware, Minnesota, Oklahoma, Tennessee
Age 5: (N = 15)	Arizona, Arkansas, Colorado, Kansas, Maine, Missouri, Nevada, New Mexico, New York, North Carolina, Ohio, Pennsylvania, South Carolina, Utah, West Virginia

Note: Based on USDOE data reported by Fraas, 1986. Service levels and populations included vary among these 41 states.

Changes to Preschool Incentive Grants

Public Law 99-457, enacted 11 years after passage of P.L. 94-142, sought to rectify this situation with preschoolers by altering the funding mechanisms for the preschool incentive grants. The old ceiling of $300 per child was eliminated; instead, states could begin to receive $300 per child in fiscal year 1987. This amount was required; it was not a ceiling. This amount increased by $100 for fiscal year 1988 and by an additional $100 in fiscal year 1989, bringing the total preschool grant per child to $500 in fiscal year 1989. Such funding is nearly a five-fold increase over the $110 provided in 1986. In fiscal year 1990, the law reinstitutes a ceiling on the per child amount of the preschool grant; federal funding cannot exceed $1,000 per child.

In addition, the law, in order to encourage states to serve all eligible preschoolers ages 3 to 5, includes a new source of funds. States may receive *up to* $3,800 per new eligible preschooler served. The actual size of this award will depend on estimates by all states of the total number of new preschoolers they will serve, and Congress estimated that approximately 70,000 such children remained unserved in 1986 (House Report 99-860). At this writing Congress is considering a change in this incentive provision. Under the law, states receive this money for increases in the number of preschoolers. In some states, due to population shifts, efforts were made to serve new preschoolers, but the total count either did not grow or declined, causing these states to receive insufficient funds.

Finally, the new law includes a limited mandate. Beginning in fiscal year 1990 *all* states must provide a free and appropriate public education to all eligible preschool handicapped children. (This mandate may be waived only for 1 year if the aggregate amount appropriated for preschool grants in fiscal years 1987 through 1989 does not reach $656 million or if the amount appropriated for these grants in fiscal year 1990 was less than $306 million.) If any state fails to provide these services by then, the law prohibits that state from receiving grant funds that may be provided to the state under Parts C through G of the Education of the Handicapped Act (see Table 1.1 for a description of these parts).

It is the expectation of Congress that these enhanced preschool incentives will result in delivery of full services to all eligible preschool children with handicaps by school year 1990–91 (or 1991–92 if the 1-year waiver is exercised) (House Report 99-860). However, the changes made by P.L. 99-457 to the Education of the Handicapped Act with respect to preschoolers are relatively minor. In essence, these changes are refinements – important ones, but nevertheless they are only refinements to Part B of the Education of the Handicapped Act. In contrast, the addition of Part H to the EHA will significantly alter the nature of early intervention services in the states. It is the Part H changes that will occupy so much of our professional attention over the next several years.

Services to Infants and Toddlers and Their Families

The addition of the infant and toddler component of P.L. 99-457 (Part H) represents a logical downward extension of federal policy for children with disabilities. When P.L. 94-142 was originally debated on the Senate floor, as S. 6, this legislation contained mandated services for preschoolers (Garwood, Fewell, & Neisworth, 1988). During floor debates, this provision was eliminated, and the optional preschool incentive grant program was instituted instead. Now, more than a decade later, under P.L. 99-457, these provisions have been strengthened, and it is likely that Part B of EHA eventually will require states to serve all eligible children with handicaps from age 3 up.

Interest in early intervention for infants and young children is not new. In the 1960s, there was a confluence of factors that directly affected the course of early intervention. One factor was the election of John Kennedy to the presidency in 1960. Kennedy had a mentally retarded sister, and his family was, and is, interested in mental retardation issues. President Kennedy was also interested in establishing programs that would help reduce the level of poverty in this country, and he created an antipoverty task force that recommended a massive community effort. Head Start was a part of this effort. It was designed to improve the cognitive and social skills of preschoolers from low-income families. In so doing, policymakers hoped that this early intervention would enable these children to break out of the "cycle of poverty." [It is worth noting that Head Start was proposed to Kennedy by a committee headed by pediatrician Robert E. Cooke, who had come into contact with the Kennedy family because of President Kennedy's mentally retarded sister (Steiner, 1976).]

Another factor promoting early intervention was the publication of two important books about human development: J. McV. Hunt's *Intelligence and Experience* (1961) and Benjamin Bloom's *Stability and Change in Human Characteristics* (1964). Both books provided evidence of the importance of the early years to later development and stimulated early intervention research and program development. In addition, the views of Jean Piaget and other developmentalists, which stressed the importance of the infant's environment on development, were increasingly becoming known to American behavioral scientists and policymakers (Garwood, 1983b). Also critical were studies that highlighted the importance of parents as critical mediators of their child's development (e.g., Bronfenbrenner, 1969; Hess & Shipman, 1965). The importance of these studies was not lost on those who were drafting P.L. 99-457.

This confluence of events helped generate massive federal support for early intervention initiatives such as Head Start. In addition, the federal government funded other early intervention projects. One example is the Parent Child Development Center project, which was a 10-year investment in studying the effects of early intervention and parent involvement on child development (Andrews et al., 1982). These events also helped to highlight the notion of "risk" for young children by emphasizing the possible negative effects of exposure to certain environmental conditions on child development.

The Concept of Risk

If exposure to certain environmental conditions could put young children at risk for subsequent development, then conversely, developmental delay might be prevented or mitigated if interventions were designed to maximize developmental potential. As example, the following conditions, considered singly or in various combinations, can put an infant's development at risk for delay:

Poverty. About 25% of all babies are born into poverty; in 1983, 3,527,000 children under 4 were living in poverty in the United States.

Single parent. In 1983, 20% of all babies born were born to single mothers, a five-fold increase since 1950.

Teenage parent. The birth rate for unmarried white adolescents is about 66% of its 1970 rate; the rate for blacks is 400% of that for whites.

Low birth weight. About 250,000 babies are born annually weighing less than 2,500 grams; of these, more than 43,000 weigh less than 1,500 grams.

Congenital anomalies. Between 100,000 and 150,000 infants are born each year with congenital anomalies that will lead to mental retardation.

Fetal alcohol. More than 3,700 infants are born annually with Fetal Alcohol Syndrome.

Failure to thrive. Failure to Thrive Syndrome (consistently below the third percentile on growth) affects 3% of the pediatric population, and is especially prevalent among infants less than 18 months of age.

Mental health. While there are no national data, a representative New York county study revealed that children under 4 represented 16% of patients diagnosed with mental health problems. Maternal depression, marital disharmony, and poor parent-child relationships positively correlated with child mental health problems.

Abuse. Infants and toddlers who are abused represent about 6% of the general population.

Nutrition. A 1982 Center for Disease Control survey of children under 2 revealed that 8.3% were under the fifth percentile for height.

Environmental poisons. About 18% of black children and 3% of white children under age 3 have elevated blood lead levels.

We are all familiar with instances in which children have developed normally despite the presence of one or more of the above factors. Unfortunately, more instances of developmental delay are known to exist, and the incidence of developmental delay increases exponentially when multiple risk factors are present. [The statistics quoted above were abstracted from *Infants Can't Wait: The Numbers*, a publication of the National Center for Clinical Infant Programs (NCCIP, 1986).]

Effective social policy at the national, state, and local levels can be instrumental in helping to eliminate risk conditions such as those summarized above. In that sense, P.L. 99-457 represents social policy that is designed to achieve this end. However, success in achieving these social policy objectives rests heavily with the ability of states and local communities to provide the types of interventions that will remove infants and toddlers and their families from conditions such as those summarized above. This ability is not only economic in nature, for availability of economic resources is critical, but this ability also refers to community interest in dealing with the problems of disability, availability of trained personnel, the presence of groups willing to advocate on behalf of young children with disabilities, and the availability of agencies willing to share limited resources with other agencies in the community.

In 1974, at a conference held at the University of North Carolina (the proceedings are published in Tjossem, 1976), national attention was focused on the importance of establishing early intervention programs for high-risk infants and young children. According to Tjossem (1976),

> prevention of mental retardation and related developmental disabilities is the ultimate goal of our national effort to combat these disorders. Significant progress toward this objective is evidenced by advances in research incorporated in improved and expanded service programs. Still, attainment of this national goal is not in sight. (p. 3)

Tjossem (1976) pointed to evaluations of programs like Head Start as providing much of what is known about the effectiveness of early intervention. He also pointed out that much less is known regarding the effects of early intervention for young children with handicaps or developmental disorders. Despite this lack of information, Tjossem argued for the importance of developing early intervention initiatives for developmentally disordered children, and he proposed a typology of risk status that has found its way into P.L. 99-457. These categories of risk are summarized in Table 1.5.

The work of this conference and the resulting publication were no doubt instrumental in encouraging research on early intervention with very young children with handicaps. For example, in the early 1980s, there was enough research being conducted so that the journal *Topics in Early Childhood Special Education* could devote three issues to reporting this research [volumes 3(1), 5(2), and 6(3)]. Other journals published similar research, much of it concluding that early intervention can be effective for young children, and the extent of its effectiveness is a function of the nature of the early intervention program, who is involved, the ages and types or severity of disabilities of the children, and other factors (see, for example, Bricker, 1982; Casto & Mastropieri, 1986; Guralnick & Bennett, 1987; Meisels, 1985; Shonkoff, Hauser-Cram, Krauss, & Upshur, 1988; White & Casto, 1985). The Department of Education has reported to Congress that:

> Studies of the effectiveness of preschool education for the handicapped have demonstrated beyond doubt the economic and educational benefits . . . for young handicapped children. In addition, studies have shown that the earlier intervention is started, the greater is the ultimate dollar savings and the higher is the rate of educational attainment by these handicapped children. (USDOE, 1985, p. xvi)

Much of this important research had been funded by the Department of Education through research initiatives contained in the EHA.

Congressional Support of Early Intervention

In 1983, when Congress enacted P.L. 98-199 to reauthorize the EHA, it included language under Part C (see Table 1.1) that gave the Secretary of Education authority to make grants to the states to assist them in planning, developing, and implementing a comprehensive delivery system for providing special education and related services to children with handicaps from birth to age 5. States could receive a *planning grant* for a maximum of 2 years to assess their needs and establish procedures to develop a state plan. Follow-

TABLE 1.5
Categories of Risk for Young Children with
Handicaps or Developmental Disorders

Category	Description
Established Risk	Infants whose early appearing atypical development is related to diagnosed medical disorders of known etiology and that have known expectancies for developmental delay as an outcome. Down Syndrome is one example; other examples include chromosomal disorders that can result in mental retardation, severe microcephaly, sensory impairments, Fetal Alcohol Syndrome, epilepsy, and inborn errors of metabolism.
Biological Risk	Infants presenting a history of prenatal, perinatal, neonatal, and early development events that indicate the possibility of biological insult(s) to the developing central nervous system. It is likely that these conditions will increase the probability of aberrant development, and early determination of these conditions is often difficult. Low birth weight is one example; others include transient dystonia and intraperiventricular hemorrhages.
Environmental Risk	Infants may be biologically sound but their early life experiences can lead to developmental delay. Such early experiences could include the quality of maternal and family care, health care, restricted opportunities for expressing adaptive behaviors, and reduced levels of physical and social stimulation. Examples could include infants of (a) poor families, (b) teenage mothers, (c) mentally retarded parents, (d) emotionally disturbed parents, and (e) parents who are addicted to drugs or alcohol.

Note: Adapted from Tjossem (1976) and House Report 99-860.

ing this, states could receive a *development grant* for a maximum of 3 years to develop a comprehensive state plan for serving this population. Finally, states could receive an *implementation grant* for a maximum of 3 years to implement and evaluate their state plan. Under this scheme, states would have had up to 8 years of grant support from the federal government if they wished to apply for this grant support.

However, at the end of the time lines specified in P.L. 98-199, there was no commitment of continued federal support of the states' early intervention activities. In addition, there were no guidelines to the states with respect to the development of an early intervention system or its components. Finally, the law allowed only up to 30% of the appropriated funds for Section 623 of Part C (Early Education for Handicapped Children). At best this language would have generated only a few million dollars for states to plan, develop, and implement early intervention services for children from birth to age 5. It is no wonder that by 1985, 27 states were in the first year of their planning grant phase and 24 were in the second year; only four states were in the development phase (USDOE, 1987). The incentives just did not seem strong enough for states to take early intervention seriously. And, as Table 1.6 shows, perhaps as a consequence, few infants were actually receiving early intervention services. According to the Department of Education's numbers, only about 36,000 infants received any sort of educational intervention in school year 1984–85. Annually in the United States about 3.4 million infants are born (NCCIP, 1986). This number of 36,000 is even less than the number of very low birth weight infants born annually; it is certainly less than the 100 to 150 thousand infants born annually with congenital anomalies.

Perhaps it was time to up the stakes, and that is what Senator Lowell Weicker did. In early 1986, Senator Weicker, an acknowledged advocate of the disabled and chairman of the Senate Subcommittee on the Handicapped, introduced legislation that would have required the states to serve all handicapped children by 1990 or lose all their EHA funding; this legislation would also have expanded the definition of handicap to include developmentally delayed children. This costly legislation passed the Senate on June 6, 1986, and was sent to the House of Representatives for its consideration.

Because there was very little debate in the Senate on their legislation, the House took a different approach. It held 7 days of hearings and listened to 50 witnesses from a variety of disability groups, parent groups, educational organizations, and local and state governments On September 16, 1986, Chairman Pat Williams of the House Subcommittee on Select Education, which has jurisdiction over special education, introduced H.R. 5520. (One of the authors of this text was the staff director of this subcommittee who was responsible for overseeing the drafting of this legislation.) This legislation was the result of 6 days of conferencing with House staff and representatives of the Council for Exceptional Children, the Association for Retarded Citizens,

TABLE 1.6
Handicapped Infants and Toddlers Birth Through Age 2 Receiving Special Education and Related Services, School Year 1984–1985

Number Served	States
None	District of Columbia, Hawaii, New Hampshire
Less than 100	Delaware, Mississippi, Missouri, Montana, Oregon, Vermont, Wyoming
101–200	Arizona, Georgia, Ohio, Utah
201–300	Connecticut, Illinois, Kansas, Maine, Nevada, New Mexico, North Carolina, North Dakota, Rhode Island, South Carolina, South Dakota, Tennessee
301–400	Arkansas, Washington
401–500	Oklahoma, West Virginia
501–600	Minnesota, Virginia
601–700	Colorado
701–800	none
801–900	Florida, Idaho, Iowa, Kentucky
901–1,000	Alaska, Louisiana, Maryland, Nebraska
1,001–2,000	California, Indiana, Michigan, Texas, Wisconsin
2,001–3,000	Alabama, Massachusetts, New Jersey
3,001–4,000	New York, Pennsylvania

Total served in the 50 states: 36,494 infants

the Coalition for Citizens with Developmental Disabilities, the American Association of School Administrators, the National School Boards Association, and the National Governors Association. In addition, House staff met with Senate staff to discuss the provisions that were to be included in H.R. 5520. On September 22, 1986, the House passed H.R. 5520; a few days later the Senate accepted this legislation without changing a word except to renumber it as S. 2294, the number originally associated with Senator Weicker's legislation. On October 8, 1986, the legislation was signed into law and officially became the 457th of the Ninety-ninth Congress, hence P.L. 99-457.

The Ninety-ninth Congress that passed P.L. 99-457 was more pragmatic and, in some ways, less controlling than earlier congresses dealing with legislation for the handicapped. Developers of P.L. 99-457 were careful to involve the states in those decisions that might be costly to them. For example, under

P.L. 99-457, it is up to the states to define what developmental delay means and to establish the objective criteria for assessing delay. Public Law 99-457 did not expand the definition of "handicap" as had the Senate bill; instead it left it up to the states to decide whether to serve young children who were at risk for developmental delay. This new law did not try to create an administrative structure for developing the early intervention system; it was up to the states to decide on the best agency to operate this new program. Despite the pragmatic and participatory nature of P.L. 99-457, the new law does specify all the components a state must establish if it is to receive federal assistance. The guidelines for developing a comprehensive early intervention system are laid down in this law.

Finally, and significantly, Part H of P.L. 99-457 carried with it $50 million to assist the states in developing their comprehensive early intervention system; this was a much stronger incentive than the relatively small amount that had been available under P.L. 98-199. Almost as soon as the funding was announced, all states and territories announced that they would participate in developing the required early intervention system for infants and toddlers and their families. In fiscal year 1988, the amount available to the states for Part H was slightly more than $67 million, and this amount is expected to increase over subsequent years.

In the remaining chapters of this book, we discuss in specific detail the components of a comprehensive early intervention system specified in Part H of P.L. 99-457. We also provide information about how these components can be implemented and documented.

2

The Law, the Report, and the Regulations

The Law. Public Law 99-457 is a reauthorization of the discretionary programs (see Table 1.1, Chapter 1, Parts C through F) that already were contained in the Education of the Handicapped Act (EHA). Part B of EHA, also known as P.L. 94-142, is permanently authorized. However, the new law also amends section 619 of EHA-Part B to strengthen the incentives for serving preschool children with handicaps, and it establishes two new discretionary programs. Part G was added to promote the use of new technology, media, and materials in the education of the handicapped. Part H, the focus of this book, establishes a program of financial assistance to states to help them develop and implement a statewide system of early intervention services for infants and toddlers and their families; Part H also specifies the minimum components of such a system. This chapter includes a reprint of Part H of the law as it was enacted on October 8, 1986.

This new law names the Secretary of Education as the administering agent; therefore, references throughout P.L. 99-457 to the Secretary refer to the Secretary of Education.

The Report. In addition this chapter reproduces portions of the Committee Report that accompanied this law. Under the rules of the House of Representatives, when legislation is referred from a committee of the House to the floor of the House for action, that legislation must be accompanied by a report explaining the intent of the legislation; thus the report is an important document because it helps to clarify what Congress intended when it wrote the law.

Typically, when the House and the Senate both pass companion pieces of legislation, members of both bodies are appointed to work out any differences in the legislation, and the report that describes that resolution is usually called the "Statement of the Managers" or the "Conference Report." However, because the Senate accepted the House version of this early intervention legislation without any change on the floor of the Senate, no conference was held, and thus, the House Report is the germane explanatory document. This report is House Report 99-860, a report to accompany the Education of the Handicapped Act Amendments of 1986.

In this chapter, portions of the report that clarify portions of Part H are interspersed with the text of the law. These portions are set off and identified as material from the report.

Regulations. When legislation is enacted and funded, the agency within the executive branch that is charged with administering the law (in the case of P.L. 99-457, the Department of Education) is required to prepare regulations that describe how the law will be carried out. These regulations must be published for public comment, and after a reasonable time, the administration can finalize the regulations and begin implementing the law. In some cases, and Part H is one of those cases, the administration will not wait on the finalization of the regulations but will implement legislation using the statute as a guide. The proposed regulations for Part H were published in the Federal Register for public comment on November 18, 1987, over 1 year after the president signed the bill into law. At this writing (late summer, 1988), the regulations have not been finalized. Thus, we reproduce the proposed regulations at the end of this chapter.

Part H: Handicapped Infants and Toddlers

FINDINGS AND POLICY

SEC. 671. (a) FINDINGS. – The Congress finds that there is an urgent and substantial need –

(1) to enhance the development of handicapped infants and toddlers and to minimize their potential for developmental delay,

(2) to reduce the educational costs to our society, including our Nation's schools, by minimizing the need for special education and related services after handicapped infants and toddlers reach school age,

(3) to minimize the likelihood of institutionalization of handicapped individuals and maximize the potential for their independent living in society, and

(4) to enhance the capacity of families to meet the special needs of their infants and toddlers with handicaps.

(b) POLICY. – It is therefore the policy of the United States to provide financial assistance to States –

(1) to develop and implement a statewide, comprehensive, coordinated, multidisciplinary, interagency program of early intervention services for handicapped infants and toddlers and their families,

(2) to facilitate the coordination of payment for early intervention services from Federal, State, local, and private sources (including public and private insurance coverage), and

(3) to enhance its capacity to provide quality early intervention services and expand and improve existing early intervention services being provided to handicapped infants, toddlers, and their families.

House Report 99-860: Background and Need for the Legislation

Because of advances in research methodology, instrumentation, and theory educators and behavioral scientists have come to view even very young infants as capable of participating in complex interactions with their world. For example, we now believe that newborns have a functioning perceptual system capable of intersensory coordination, that they are capable of making multiple categorizations, that they possess both central and peripheral vision at birth, can coordinate visual and auditory input by age 2½ months, show evidence of recognition memory by 4 months, and are able to recognize relatively abstract two-dimensional stimuli by 5 months.

Infants are also competent and capable of exhibiting complex and voluntary motor activity much earlier than once thought. For example, researchers have found that infants as young as 12 months of age were able to use pointing behavior to call interesting objects to the attention of others, . . . Thus, social competence can develop very early in life.

However, in addition to participating in social relationships, infants are also capable of initiating and maintaining social interactions at a very early age. There is clear evidence to suggest that sociable infants are capable of eliciting more stimulation from care-givers and that this heightened social competence leads to accelerated cognitive development.

Thus, the infant's developing physical, cognitive, and social competencies are very important. Because of our recognition of the early appearance of these and other competencies, infants increasingly are being viewed as active organizers of their experience and not as passive and helpless creatures. Likewise, such recognition has also made it more feasible and tenable to develop early successful intervention approaches for handicapped infants and toddlers.

The Committee therefore concludes that an overwhelming case exists for expanding and improving the provision of early intervention and preschool programs (pp. 4–5).

More specifically, testimony and research indicate that early intervention and preschool services accomplish the following:

(1) help enhance intelligence in some children:

(2) produce substantial gains in physical development, cognitive development, language and speech development, psychosocial development and self-help skills;

(3) help prevent the development of secondary handicapping conditions;

(4) reduce family stress;

(5) reduce societal dependency and institutionalization;

(6) reduce the need for special class placement in special education programs once the children reach school age; and

(7) save substantial costs to society and our nation's schools (p. 5).

DEFINITIONS

SEC. 672. As used in this part—

(1) The term "handicapped infants and toddlers" means individuals from birth [through] age 2, inclusive, who need early intervention services because they—

(A) are experiencing developmental delays, as measured by appropriate diagnostic instruments and procedures in one or more of the following areas: Cognitive development, physical development, language and speech development, psychosocial development, or self-help skills, or

(B) have a diagnosed physical or mental condition which has a high probability of resulting in developmental delay. Such term may also include, at a state's discretion, individuals from birth [through] age 2, inclusive, who are at risk of having substantial developmental delays if early intervention services are not provided.

(2) "Early intervention services" are developmental services which—

(A) are provided under public supervision,

(B) are provided at no cost except where Federal or State law provides for a system of payments by families, including a schedule of sliding fees,

(C) are designed to meet a handicapped infant's or toddler's developmental needs in any one or more of the following areas:

(i) physical development,

(ii) cognitive development,

(iii) language and speech development,

(iv) psychosocial development, or

(v) self-help skills,

(D) meet the standards of the state, including the requirements of this part,

(E) include—

(i) family training, counseling, and home visits,

(ii) special instruction,

(iii) speech pathology and audiology,

(iv) occupational therapy,

(v) physical therapy,

(vi) psychological services,

(vii) case management services,

(viii) medical services only for diagnostic or evaluation purposes,

(ix) early identification, screening, and assessment services, and

(x) health services necessary to enable the infant or toddler to benefit from the other early intervention services,

(F) are provided by qualified personnel, including

(i) special educators,

(ii) speech and language pathologists and audiologists,

(iii) occupational therapists,

(iv) physical therapists,

(v) psychologists,

(vi) social workers,

(vii) nurses,

(viii) nutritionists, and

(G) are provided in conformity with an individualized family service plan adopted in accordance with section 677.

(3) The term "developmental delay" has the meaning given such term by a State under section 676(b)(1).

(4) The term "Council" means the State Interagency Coordinating Council established under section 682.

House Report 99-860: Definitions

The phrase "birth [through] age two, inclusive" means infants and toddlers from birth until they reach their third birthday. However, this provision shall not be construed to prohibit an agency from continuing to provide services where a child turns three during the summer and services provided by a local educational agency do not commence until September. Where the local provider of early intervention services and the local educational agency are not the same, it is essential that the agencies coordinate their efforts to transition the child to the special education system operated by the local educational agency (p. 6).

The phrase "have a diagnosed physical or mental condition which has a high probability of resulting in developmental delay" is included to enable States to serve categories of infants and toddlers who will need early interven-

tion services even though many will not exhibit developmental delays at the time of diagnosis.

Examples include: Down Syndrome and other chromosomal abnormalities which are likely to result in mental retardation; severe microcephaly; Cornelia de Lange Syndrome; sensory impairments; Rubenstein-Taybi Syndrome; Fetal Alcohol Syndrome; Epilepsy: and Inborn Errors of Metabolism.

The term may also include at a State's discretion, individuals from birth through age two, inclusive, who are "at risk" of having substantial developmental delays if early intervention services are not provided. The phrase "at risk" includes infants and toddlers who are not otherwise covered by the general definition described above. See Tjossem, Theodore. Early Intervention: Issues and Approaches. In Tjossem, T., ed. Intervention Strategies for High Risk and Handicapped Children. Baltimore, University Park Press, 1976.

The term "developmental delay" has the meaning given such term by a State. In providing this discretion to the States, the Committee wishes to emphasize that it is not our intent to permit a State to totally ignore or establish standards of measurement or other definitional provisions that preclude addressing any one of the five developmental areas included in the definition. Thus, it is expected that the definition will encompass levels of functioning in all five developmental areas.

The term "early intervention services" means developmental services which satisfy seven criteria. First, such services are provided under public supervision. This means that ultimate responsibility for the provision of services remains with the lead agency designated or established by the Governor. The fact that ultimate responsibility rests with the lead agency should not be construed in any way to limit the agency's authority to make arrangements with local service providers (public and private) who in turn may contract or make arrangements with others for the provision of services (p. 7).

The early intervention services included in the bill are not meant to be exhaustive; rather they are intended to be illustrative of the types of services a handicapped infant or toddler may receive under this program (p. 8).

The phrase "case management services" includes services provided to families of handicapped infants and toddlers to assist them in gaining access to early intervention services and other services identified in the infant or toddler's individualized family service plan; to ensure timely delivery of available services; and to coordinate the provision of early intervention services with other services (such as medical services for other than diagnostic and evaluation purposes) which the infant or toddler needs or is being provided.

The Committee intends that case management be an active, ongoing process of continuously seeking the appropriate services or situations to benefit the development of each infant or toddler being served for the duration of each child's eligibility.

Specific case management services include: coordinating the performance of evaluations; assisting families in identifying available service providers; participating in the development of the IFSP [the individualized family service plan], coordinating and monitoring the delivery of available services; informing families of the availability of advocacy services available to the family; coordinating with the medical and health providers and facilitating the development of a transition plan to preschool services, where appropriate.

The term "health services necessary to benefit from other early intervention services" does not include such services as: surgical or purely medical procedures such as cleft palate surgery; surgery for club foot; management of congenital heart ailments; management of cystic fibrosis; and shunting of hydrocephalus (p. 8).

(E)arly intervention services are provided in conformity with an individualized family service plan, except that because infant development is relatively rapid and therefore undue delay could be potentially harmful, such services may commence before the completion of the initial plan with the parent's consent (p. 8).

GENERAL AUTHORITY

SEC. 673. The Secretary shall, in accordance with this part, make grants to States (from their allocations under section 684) to assist each State to develop a statewide, comprehensive, coordinated, multidisciplinary, interagency system to provide early intervention services to handicapped infants and toddlers and their families.

House Report 99-860: General Authority

This program is designed to build upon existing State systems of serving handicapped infants and toddlers and to facilitate the development of systems in States desiring to serve this population (p. 8).

GENERAL ELIGIBILITY

SEC. 674. In order to be eligible for a grant under section 673 for any fiscal year, a State shall demonstrate to the Secretary (in its application under section 678) that the State has established a State Interagency Coordinating Council which meets the requirements of section 682.

CONTINUING ELIGIBILITY

SEC. 675. (a) FIRST TWO YEARS. – In order to be eligible for a grant under section 673 for the first or second year of a State's participation under this part, a State shall include in its application under section 678 for that year assurances that funds received under section 673 shall be used to assist the State to plan, develop, and implement the statewide system required by section 676.

(b) THIRD AND FOURTH YEAR. – (1) In order to be eligible for a grant under section 673 for a third or fourth year of a State's participation under this part, a State shall include in its application under section 678 for that year information and assurances demonstrating to the satisfaction of the Secretary that –

(A) the State has adopted a policy which incorporates all of the components of a statewide system in accordance with section 676 or obtained a waiver from the Secretary under paragraph (2),

(B) funds shall be used to plan, develop, and implement the statewide system required by section 676, and

(C) such statewide system will be in effect no later than the beginning of the fourth year of the State's participation under section 673, except that with respect to section 676(b)(4), a State need only conduct multidisciplinary assessments, develop individualized family service plans, and make available case management services.

(2) Notwithstanding paragraph (1), the Secretary may permit a State to continue to receive assistance under section 673 during such third year even if the State has not adopted the policy required by paragraph (1)(A) before receiving assistance if the State demonstrates in its application –

(A) that the State has made a good faith effort to adopt such a policy,

(B) the reasons why it was unable to meet the timeline and the steps remaining before such a policy will be adopted, and

(C) an assurance that the policy will be adopted and go into effect before the fourth year of such assistance.

(c) FIFTH AND SUCCEEDING YEARS. – In order to be eligible for a grant under section 673 for a fifth and any succeeding year of a State's participation under this part, a State shall include in its application under section 678 for that year information and assurances demonstrating to the satisfaction of the Secretary that the State has in effect the statewide system required by section 676 and a description of services to be provided under section 676(b)(2).

(d) EXCEPTION. – Notwithstanding subsections (a) and (b), a State which has in effect a State law, enacted before September 1, 1986, that requires the provision of free appropriate public education to handicapped children from birth through age 2, inclusive, shall be eligible for a grant under section 673 for the first through fourth years of a State's participation under this part.

House Report 99-860: Continuing Eligibility

It is expected that funds will be used under this part for the first three years to accomplish many of the same objectives expected to have been accomplished under the planning, development and implementation grants authorized under section 623(b) of current law [see Chapter 1 for a discussion of this issue].

In order to be eligible for a grant under part H for the third year of a State's participation, a State must include information and assurances demonstrating that the State has adopted a policy which incorporated all of the components of a statewide system of early intervention services (unless the State has obtained a waiver from the Secretary).

The statewide system must be in effect . . . before the beginning of the fourth year. With respect to the development and implementation of an individualized family service plan . . . , in the fourth year the State need only: conduct multidisciplinary assessments, develop individualized family service plans, and make available case management services. Other early intervention services need not be made available to all handicapped infants and toddlers until the beginning of the fifth year of a State's participation in the program.

It is expected that the State application will include all of the policies constituting the statewide system. This requirement may be satisfied by including a copy of the applicable statute or regulations.

The Secretary may permit a State to continue to receive assistance for the third year even if it has not adopted the policy establishing the statewide system if the State demonstrates that it has made a good faith effort to adopt such a policy, the reasons for its failure and the steps it will take to ensure its adoption, and an assurance that the policy will go into effect before the beginning of the fourth year (p. 9).

COMPONENTS OF A STATEWIDE SYSTEM

SEC. 676. (a) IN GENERAL. – A statewide system of coordinated, comprehensive, multidisciplinary, interagency programs providing appropriate early intervention services to all handicapped infants and toddlers and their families shall include the minimum components under subsection (b).

(b) MINIMUM COMPONENTS. — The statewide system required by subsection (a) shall include, at a minimum —

(1) a definition of the term "developmentally delayed" that will be used by the State in carrying out programs under this part,

(2) timetables for ensuring that appropriate early intervention services will be available to all handicapped infants and toddlers in the State before the beginning of the fifth year of a State's participation under this part,

(3) a timely, comprehensive, multidisciplinary evaluation of the functioning of each handicapped infant and toddler in the State and the needs of the families to appropriately assist in the development of the handicapped infant or toddler,

(4) for each handicapped infant and toddler in the State, an individualized family service plan in accordance with section 677, including case management services in accordance with such service plan,

(5) a comprehensive child find system, consistent with Part B, including a system for making referrals to service providers that includes timeliness and provides for the participation by primary referral sources,

(6) a public awareness program focusing on early intervention of handicapped infants and toddlers,

(7) a central directory which includes early intervention services, resources, and experts available in the State and research and demonstration projects being conducted in the State,

(8) a comprehensive system of personnel development,

(9) a single line of responsibility in a lead agency designated or established by the Governor for carrying out —

(A) the general administration, supervision, and monitoring of programs and activities receiving assistance under section 673 to ensure compliance with this part,

(B) the identification and coordination of all available resources within the State from Federal, State, local and private resources,

(C) the assignment of financial responsibility to the appropriate agency,

(D) the development of procedures to ensure that services are provided to handicapped infants and toddlers and their families in a timely manner pending the resolution of any disputes among public agencies or service providers,

(E) the resolution of intra- and interagency disputes, and

(F) the entry into formal interagency agreements that define the financial responsibility of each agency for paying for early intervention services (consistent with State law) and procedures for resolving disputes and that include all additional components necessary to ensure meaningful cooperation and coordination,

(10) a policy pertaining to the contracting or making of other arrangements with service providers to provide early intervention services in the

State, consistent with the provisions of this part, including the contents of the application used and the conditions of the contract or other arrangements,

(11) a procedure for securing timely reimbursement of funds used under this part in accordance with section 681(a),

(12) procedural safeguards with respect to programs under this part as required by section 680,

(13) policies and procedures relating to the establishment and maintenance of standards to ensure that personnel necessary to carry out this part are appropriately and adequately prepared and trained, including –

(A) the establishment and maintenance of standards which are consistent with any State approved or recognized certification, licensing, registration, or other comparable requirements which apply to the area in which such personnel are providing early intervention services, and

(B) to the extent such standards are not based on the highest requirements in the State applicable to a specific profession or discipline, the steps the State is taking to require the retraining or hiring of personnel that meet appropriate professional requirements in the State, and

(14) a system for compiling data on the number of handicapped infants and toddlers and their families in the State in need of appropriate early intervention services (which may be based on a sampling of data), the number of such infants and toddlers and their families served, the types of services provided (which may be based on a sampling of data), and other information required by the Secretary.

House Report 99-860: Components of a Statewide System

(With respect to component five), "Primary referral sources" include hospitals, physicians, other health care providers, public health facilities, and day care facilities.

The Committee recognizes [that] the existing and long established child find procedures established under part B [of EHA] may be an appropriate vehicle for satisfying this requirement. However, such procedures must be modified or expanded (if necessary) to include a system of referrals and the system must include timelines and provide for the participation by primary referral sources (p. 10).

(T)he system must include a comprehensive system of personnel development. The system must include training of public and private service providers, primary referral sources, and persons who will provide services after receiving such training. Services and training may be provided directly by the State or through a grant, contract or other arrangement with other entities.

The Committee believes that this component is one of the most important in the system. Without qualified personnel, services will not affect the successes envisioned by the program. To the extent that a State's current system of personnel development established under part B [of EHA] already includes the training of personnel described above to provide early intervention services, consistent with this part, such a State would be considered in compliance with this section.

———————

(T)he system must include a single line of authority in a lead agency designated or established by the Governor to carry out: the general administration, supervision, and monitoring of programs and activities; the identification and coordination of all available resources within the State from Federal, State, local and private sources and the assignment of financial responsibility to the appropriate State agency; the resolution of State interagency disputes and procedures for ensuring the provision of services pending the resolution of such disputes; and the entering into [of] formal State interagency agreements that define the financial responsibility of each State agency for paying for early intervention services (consistent with State law) and include, among other things, procedures for resolving disputes.

Without this critical requirement, there is an abdication of responsibility for the provision of early intervention services for handicapped infants and toddlers. Although the bill recognizes the importance of interagency responsibility for providing or paying for appropriate services, it is essential that ultimate responsibility remain in a lead agency so that buck-passing among State agencies does not occur to the detriment of the handicapped infant or toddler (p. 11).

In States serving significant numbers of Indian handicapped infants and toddlers, the lead agency must consult with and obtain input from Tribal education offices/committees, BIA [Bureau of Indian Affairs, Department of the Interior] schools, tribal schools, Head Start programs and other providers of service at the local and State level to ensure that the needs of these infants and toddlers are considered and accounted for in the statewide system.

(T)he system must include a policy pertaining to the contracting or making of other arrangements with local service providers, i.e., those entities with which the State makes arrangements for, among other things, the infant or toddler's assessment; the development of an individualized family service plan; and the provision of services. The policy must include the contents of the application used and the conditions of the contract or other arrangement.

It is the Committee's intent that the policy developed by the State must be consistent with the provisions of this part. Thus, for example, it is the

Committee's intent that an individualized family service plan developed by a local service provider will be consistent with the provisions of section 677 of part H (p. 11).

INDIVIDUALIZED FAMILY SERVICE PLAN

SEC. 677. (a) ASSESSMENT AND PROGRAM DEVELOPMENT. – Each handicapped infant or toddler and the infant or toddler's family shall receive –

(1) a multidisciplinary assessment of unique needs and the identification of services appropriate to meet such needs, and

(2) a written individualized family service plan developed by a multidisciplinary team, including the parent or guardian, as required by subsection (d).

(b) PERIODIC REVIEW. – The individualized family service plan shall be evaluated once a year and the family shall be provided a review of the plan at 6-month intervals (or more often where appropriate based on infant and toddler and family needs).

(c) PROMPTNESS AFTER ASSESSMENT. – The individualized family service plan shall be developed within a reasonable time after the assessment required by subsection (a)(1) is completed. With the parent's consent, early intervention services may commence prior to the completion of such assessment.

(d) CONTENT OF PLAN. – The individualized family service plan shall be in writing and contain –

(1) a statement of the infant's or toddler's present levels of physical development, cognitive development, language and speech development, psychosocial development, and self-help skills, based on acceptable objective criteria,

(2) a statement of the family's strengths and needs relating to enhancing the development of the family's handicapped infant or toddler,

(3) a statement of the major outcomes expected to be achieved for the infant and toddler and the family, and the criteria, procedures, and time lines used to determine the degree to which progress toward achieving the outcomes are being made and whether modifications or revisions of the outcomes or services are necessary,

(4) a statement of specific early intervention services necessary to meet the unique needs of the infant or toddler and the family, including the frequency, intensity, and the method of delivering services,

(5) the projected dates for initiation of services and the anticipated duration of such services,

(6) the name of the case manager from the profession most immediately relevant to the infant's and toddler's or family's needs who will be responsible for the implementation of the plan and coordination with other agencies and persons, and

(7) the steps to be taken supporting the transition of the handicapped toddler to services provided under part B to the extent such services are considered appropriate.

House Report 99-860: Individualized Family Service Plan

(E)ach handicapped infant or toddler and the infant's or toddler's family must receive a multidisciplinary assessment of unique needs and the identification of services appropriate to meet such needs and a written individualized family service plan developed by a multidisciplinary team, which includes the parents or guardian. The Committee wishes to make it clear that the parents or guardian may decide to invite someone to the meeting to assist them present their positions.

(T)he individualized family service plan must be evaluated at least once a year and the family must be provided a review of the plan at least at 6-month intervals (or more often where appropriate based on infant, toddler, and family needs) to determine the degree to which progress toward achieving the outcomes [is] being made and whether modifications or revisions of outcomes or services are necessary.

(T)he individualized family service plan must be developed within a reasonable time after assessment. However, with the parent's consent, early intervention services may commence prior to the completion of the assessment. [Exercise of t]he authority to allow services to commence prior to the completion of the assessment should be the exception and not the rule. Further, this authority should not be used as a means for systematically circumventing the obligation to complete the assessment and develop the plan within a reasonable time.

(T)he individualized family service plan must be in writing and contain the following statements and information. First, a statement of the infant's or toddler's present levels of physical development, cognitive development, language and speech development, psychosocial development, and self-help skills based on professionally acceptable objective criteria. Second, a statement of the family's strengths [emphasis added] and needs relating to enhancing the development of the family's handicapped infant or toddler.

Third, a statement of the major outcomes expected to be achieved for the infant or toddler and the family; the criteria, procedures, and time lines used to determine the degree to which progress toward achieving the outcomes is being made and whether modifications or revisions of the outcomes or services are necessary.

Fourth, a statement of specific early intervention services necessary to meet the unique needs of the infant and toddler and the family, including the frequency and intensity and method of delivering services. Fifth, the projected date for initiation of services and the anticipated duration of such services.

Sixth, the name of the case manager from the profession most immediately relevant to the infant's or toddler's or family's needs who will be responsible for the implementation of the plan and coordination with other agencies and persons.

Finally, the steps to be taken supporting the transition of the handicapped infant or toddler to services provided under part B of the Act to the extent special education and related services are considered appropriate. Thus, steps to transition the child are unnecessary if the child, as a result of early intervention services, does not require special education and related services.

The Committee wishes to emphasize that the provision regarding the individualized family service plan does not require that any agency or person be held accountable if an infant or toddler does not achieve the growth projected, i.e., the plan does not constitute a guarantee of results. However, agencies and persons are not relieved of the responsibility of making good faith efforts to assist the infant or toddler in achieving the outcomes [nor does a parent lose the] right to complain if the parent feels that these efforts are not being made (pp. 12–13).

STATE APPLICATIONS AND ASSURANCES

SEC. 678. (a) APPLICATION. – Any State desiring to receive a grant under section 673 for any year shall submit an application to the Secretary at such time and in such manner as the Secretary may reasonably require by regulation. Such an application shall contain –

(1) a designation of the lead agency in the State that will be responsible for the administration of funds provided under section 673,

(2) information demonstrating eligibility of the State under section 674,

(3) the information or assurances required to demonstrate eligibility of the State or the particular year of participation under section 675, and

(4) (A) information demonstrating that the State has provided (i) public hearings, (ii) adequate notice of such hearings, and (iii) an opportunity for comment to the general public before the submission of such application and before the adoption by the State of the policies described in such application, and (B) a summary of the public comments and the State's responses.

(5) a description of the uses for which funds will be expended in accordance with this part and for the fifth and succeeding fiscal years, a description of the services to be provided,

(6) a description of the procedure used to ensure an equitable distribution of resources made available under this part among all geographic areas within the State, and

(7) such other information and assurances as the Secretary may reasonably require by regulation.

(b) STATEMENT OF ASSURANCES. – Any State desiring to receive a grant under section 673 shall file with the Secretary a statement at such time and in such manner as the Secretary may reasonably require by regulation. Such statement shall –

(1) assure that funds paid to the State under section 673 will be expended in accordance with this part,

(2) contain assurances that the State will comply with the requirements of section 681,

(3) provide satisfactory assurance that the control of funds provided under section 673, and title to property derived therefrom, shall be in a public agency for the uses and purposes provided in this part and that a public agency will administer such funds and property,

(4) provide for (A) making such reports in such form and containing such information as the Secretary may reasonably require to carry out the Secretary's functions under this part, and (B) keeping such records and affording access thereto as the Secretary may find necessary to assure the correctness and verification of such reports and proper disbursements of Federal funds under this part,

(5) provide satisfactory assurance that Federal funds made available under section 673 (A) will not be commingled with State funds, and (B) will be so used as to supplement and increase the level of State and local funds expended for handicapped infants and toddlers and their families and in no case to supplant such State and local funds,

(6) provide satisfactory assurance that such fiscal control and fund accounting procedures will be adopted as may be necessary to assure proper disbursement of, and accounting for, Federal funds paid under section 673 to the State, and

(7) such other information and assurances as the Secretary may reasonably require by regulation.

(c) APPROVAL OF APPLICATION AND ASSURANCES REQUIRED. – No State may receive a grant under section 673 unless the Secretary has approved the application and statement of assurances of that State. The Secretary shall not disapprove such an application or statement of assurances unless the Secretary determines after notice and opportunity for a hearing, that the application or statement of assurances fails to comply with the requirements of this section.

House Report 99-860: State Applications and Assurances

With respect to the application, the State must include, among other things, information demonstrating that the State has provided public hearings, adequate notice of such hearings, and an oppoortunity for comment to the general public before the submission of such application and before the adop-

tion by the State of the policies described in such application, and a summary of the public's comments and the State's responses. It is the Committee's intent that public input be obtained prior to the formulation of a State policy, and not simply serve as a rubber stamp for such a policy.

The application must also describe the procedure used to ensure an equitable distribution of resources made available under part H among all geographic areas within the State. The State must also submit a statement of assurances, which may be submitted once and remain on file with the Secretary and be revised only when considered necessary by the Secretary (p. 13).

USES OF FUNDS

SEC. 679. In addition to using funds provided under section 673 to plan, develop, and implement the statewide system required by section 676, a State may use such funds —

(1) for direct services for handicapped infants and toddlers that are not otherwise provided from other public or private sources, and

(2) to expand and improve on services for handicapped infants and toddlers that are otherwise available.

PROCEDURAL SAFEGUARDS

SEC. 680. The procedural safeguards required to be included in a statewide system under section 676(b)(12) shall provide, at a minimum, the following:

(1) The timely administrative resolution of complaints by parents. Any party aggrieved by the findings and decision regarding an administrative complaint shall have the right to bring a civil action with respect to the complaint, which action may be brought in any State court of competent jurisdiction or in a district court of the United States without regard to the amount in controversy. In any action brought under this paragraph, the court shall grant such relief as the court determined is appropriate.

(2) The right to confidentiality of personally identifiable information.

(3) The opportunity for parents and a guardian to examine records relating to assessment, screening, eligibility determinations, and the development and implementation of the individualized family service plan.

(4) Procedures to protect the rights of the handicapped infant and toddler whenever the parents or guardian of the child are not known, or unavailable or the child is a ward of the State, including the assignment of an individual (who shall not be an employee of the State agency providing services) to act as a surrogate for the parents or guardian.

(5) Written prior notice to the parents or guardian of the handicapped infant or toddler whenever the State agency or service provider proposes to initiate or change or refuses to initiate or change the identification,

evaluation, placement, or the provision of appropriate early intervention services to the handicapped infant or toddler.

(6) Procedures designed to assure that the notice required by paragraph (5) fully informs the parents or guardian, in the parents' or guardian's native language, unless it clearly is not feasible to do so, of all procedures available pursuant to this section.

(7) During the pendency of any proceeding or action involving a complaint, unless the State agency and the parents or guardian can otherwise agree, the child shall continue to receive the appropriate early intervention services currently being provided or if applying for initial service shall receive the services not in dispute.

House Report 99-860: Procedural Safeguards

Procedural safeguards . . . must provide, at a minimum, for: the timely resolution of administrative complaints by parents and the right to appeal to State and Federal court; the right to confidentiality of personally identifiable information; the opportunity to examine records; procedures to protect the rights of the handicapped infant and toddler whenever the parents or guardian of the child are not known, unavailable or the child is a ward of the State, including the assignment of a surrogate; and written prior notice to the parents or guardian under specified circumstances; procedures to ensure that the notice is in the parents' or guardian's native language, and procedures to ensure the provision of services pending the resolution of the complaint.

The Committee wishes to emphasize that there are two types of complaints a parent might file under this part. The first type includes complaints concerning the State's compliance with those sections of the law applicable to the parents' or guardian's particular infant or toddler. For example, a parent's complaint might assert a failure to perform the appropriate assessment; a failure to develop an appropriate individualized family service plan; or a failure to make available a particular early intervention service specified in the individualized family service plan, such as special instruction [essentially this refers to special education services].

It is the committee's intent that the procedure for resolving this category of complaints include the presentation and examination of all information relevant to the issues and a presentation of relevant viewpoints before an impartial individual with knowledge of the law and the needs of, and services available for, handicapped infants and toddlers.

It is also the Committee's intent that the procedures developed by the State result in speedy resolution of complaints because an infant's development is rapid and therefore undue delay could be potentially harmful. Thus, it would be acceptable for the impartial individual to attempt to mediate the complaint. However, if such an attempt is unsuccessful, it would be expected that the record be retained and that the decision be in writing to allow a parent who is so inclined, to appeal to the courts.

The Secretary may approve any system that includes the full set of procedural safeguards contained in part B.

The second type of complaint includes more systemic issues such as the State's failure to develop a statewide system which includes the components set out in new section 676 of the Act. This would include the failure to develop an impartial system for resolving complaints. It is the Committee's intent that the procedure for resolving this category of complaints must be consistent with the system described in the Education Department General Administration Regulation (34 CFR 76.780 et seq.). Of course, it is also expected that the Department of Education will develop procedures for resolving parental complaints of the systemic type described above (pp. 14–15).

PAYER OF LAST RESORT

SEC. 681. (a) NONSUBSTITUTION. – Funds provided under section 673 may not be used to satisfy a financial commitment for services which would have been paid for from another public or private source but for the enactment of this part, except that whenever considered necessary to prevent the delay in the receipt of appropriate early intervention services by the infant or toddler or family in a timely fashion, funds provided under section 673 may be used to pay the provider of services pending reimbursement from the agency which has ultimate responsibility for the payment.

(b) REDUCTION OF OTHER BENEFITS. – Nothing in this part shall be construed to permit the State to reduce medical or other assistance available or to alter eligibility under Title V of the Social Security Act (relating to maternal and child health) or title XIX of the Social Security Act (relating to Medicaid for handicapped infants and toddlers) within the State.

House Report 99-860: Payer of Last Resort

Funds provided under part H may not be used to satisfy a financial commitment for services which would have been paid from another public or private source but for the enactment of this part. However, the State may use part H funds to pay the provider of such services pending reimbursement by the agency which has ultimate responsibility for the payment whenever considered necessary to prevent the delay in the receipt of the appropriate early intervention services by the handicapped infant or toddler. The State must develop a procedure for securing timely reimbursement as part of the statewide system.

Consistent with the above requirement, new section 681 also specifies that nothing in part H should be construed to permit the State to reduce medical or other assistance available or to alter eligibility (to the detriment of handicapped infants or toddlers) under title V [of the Social Security Act] (relating to maternal and child health) or title XIX of the Social Security Act (relating to Medicaid for handicapped infants and toddlers) within the State.

It is the intent of Congress that the enactment of this legislation should not be construed as a license to any agency (including the lead agency and other agencies in the State), to withdraw funding for services that currently are or would be made available to handicapped infants and toddlers but for the existence of this legislation. Rather, the Committee intends to provide the impetus to facilitate interagency agreements with respect to service delivery to handicapped infants and toddlers and their families.

Thus, it is our intent that other funding sources continue; that there be greater coordination among agencies regarding the payment of costs; and that funds made available under part H be used only for direct services for handicapped infants and toddlers that are not otherwise provided from other public or private sources and to expand and improve on services that are not otherwise available (p. 15).

STATE INTERAGENCY COORDINATING COUNCIL

SEC. 682. (a) ESTABLISHMENT. – (1) Any State which desires to receive financial assistance under section 673 shall establish a State Interagency Coordinating Council composed of 15 members.

(2) The Council and the chairperson of the Council shall be appointed by the Governor. In making appointments to the Council, the Governor shall ensure that the membership of the council reasonably represents the population of the State.

(b) COMPOSITION. – The Council shall be composed of –

(1) at least 3 parents of handicapped infants or toddlers or handicapped children aged 3 through 6, inclusive,

(2) at least 3 public or private providers of early intervention services,

(3) at least one representative from the State legislature,

(4) at least one person involved in personnel preparation,

(5) other members representing each of the appropriate agencies involved in the provision of or payment for early intervention services to handicapped infants and toddlers and their families and others selected by the Governor.

(c) MEETINGS. – The Council shall meet at least quarterly and in such places as it deems necessary. The meetings shall be publicly announced, and, to the extent appropriate, open and accessible to the general public.

(d) MANAGEMENT AUTHORITY. – Subject to the approval of the Governor, the council may prepare and approve a budget using funds under this part to hire staff, and obtain the services of such professional, technical, and clerical personnel as may be necessary to carry out its functions under this part.

(e) FUNCTIONS OF COUNCIL. – The Council shall –

(1) advise and assist the lead agency designated or established under section 676(b)(9) in the performance of the responsibilities set out in such section, particularly the identification of the sources of fiscal and other support for services for early intervention programs, assignment of financial responsibility to the appropriate agency, and the promotion of the interagency agreements,

(2) advise and assist the lead agency in the preparation of applications and amendments thereto, and

(3) prepare and submit an annual report to the Governor and to the Secretary on the status of early intervention programs for handicapped infants and toddlers and their families operated within the State.

(f) CONFLICT OF INTEREST. – No member of the council shall cast a vote on any matter which would provide direct financial benefit to that member or otherwise give the appearance of a conflict of interest under State law.

(g) USE OF EXISTING COUNCILS. – to the extent that a State has established a Council before September 1, 1986, that is comparable to the Council described in this section, such Council shall be considered to be in compliance with this section. Within 4 years after the date the State accepts funds under section 673, such State shall establish a council that complies in full with this section.

House Report 99-860: State Interagency Coordinating Council

It is the Committee's expectation that the Council will play a central role in accomplishing the purposes of this part. The Committee recognizes that State level interagency cooperation has been instrumental in the successes which have been achieved in meeting the needs of handicapped infants and toddlers and such cooperation is essential. Thus, for example, the Council must provide meaningful advice and assist the lead agency [to] develop and implement the policies constituting the statewide system of coordinated, comprehensive, multidisciplinary programs under which appropriate early intervention services [are provided] to handicapped infants and toddlers and their families. Further, the persons representing the State agencies should have sufficient authority to represent the agency. The appointment of representatives of primary referral sources should facilitate the effective functioning of the Council (pp. 15–16).

FEDERAL ADMINISTRATION

SEC. 683. Sections 616, 617, and 620 shall, to the extent not inconsistent with this part, apply to the program authorized by this part except that —

(1) any reference to a State educational agency shall be deemed to be a reference to the State agency established or designated under section 676(b)(9).

(2) any reference to the education of handicapped children and the education of all handicapped children and the provision of free public education to all handicapped children shall be deemed to be a reference to the provision of services to handicapped infants and toddlers in accordance with this part, and

(3) any reference to local educational agencies and intermediate educational agencies shall be deemed to be a reference to local service providers under this part.

ALLOCATION OF FUNDS

SEC. 684. (a) From the sums appropriated to carry out this part for any fiscal year, the Secretary may reserve 1 percent for payments to Guam, American Samoa, the Virgin Islands, the Republic of the Marshall Islands, the Federated States of Micronesia, the Republic of Palau, and the Commonwealth of the Northern Mariana Islands in accordance with their respective needs.

(b) (1) The Secretary shall make payments to the Secretary of the Interior according to the need for such assistance for the provision of early intervention services to handicapped infants and toddlers and their families on reservations serviced by the elementary and secondary schools operated for Indians by the Department of the Interior. The amount of such payment for any fiscal year shall be 1.25 percent of the aggregate of the amount available to all States under this part for that fiscal year.

(2) the Secretary of the Interior may receive an allotment under paragraph (1) only after submitting to the Secretary an application which meets the requirements of section 678 and which is approved by the Secretary. Section 616 shall apply to any such application.

(c) (1) For each of the fiscal years 1987 through 1991 from the funds remaining after the reservation and payments under subsection (a) and (b), the Secretary shall allot to each State an amount which bears the same ratio to the amount of such remainder as the number of infants and toddlers in all States, except that no State shall receive less than 0.5 percent of such remainder.

(2) For the purpose of paragraph (1) —

(A) the terms "infants" and "toddlers" mean children from birth to age 3, inclusive, and

(B) the term "State" does not include the jurisdictions described in subsection (a).

(d) If any State elects not to receive its allotment under subsection (c)(1), the Secretary shall reallot, among the remaining States, amounts from such State in accordance with such subsection.

House Report 99-860: Allocation of Funds

(T)he Secretary shall allot to each State an amount which bears the same ratio to the amount of such remainder as the number of infants and toddlers in the State bears to the number of infants and toddlers in all States, except that no State may receive less than 0.5 percent. The Committee fully expects to review the use of census data for making the allocation among States when the Congress reauthorizes this part in five years. Particular consideration will be given to the use of child count procedures comparable to those used under part B (p. 16).

[With respect to handicapped infants and toddlers and their families who are Indians] (t)he Committee expects that interagency agreements will be entered into among appropriate agencies such as Indian Health Service, BIA Social Services, BIA Office of Education and the Department of Education. Too often handicapped Indians are "lost in the bureaucratic shuffle" while a determination is being made as to who is responsible for which services. Special attention is to be given in these interagency agreements to the use of home-bound teachers and utilization of a strong family based component (p. 16).

AUTHORIZATION OF APPROPRIATIONS

SEC. 685. There are authorized to be appropriated to carry out this part $50,000,000 for fiscal year 1987, $75,000,000 for fiscal year 1988, and such sums as may be necessary for each of the 3 succeeding fiscal years.

The Proposed Regulations Implementing Part H

Subpart A – General
Purposes, Eligibility, and Other General Provisions
303.1 Purpose of the early intervention program for infants and toddlers with handicaps.

The purpose of this part is to provide financial assistance to States –

(a) To develop and implement a statewide, comprehensive, coordinated, multidisciplinary, interagency program of early intervention services for infants and toddlers with handicaps and their families;

(b) To facilitate the coordination of payment for early intervention services from Federal, State, local, and private sources (including public and private insurance coverage); and

(c) To enhance the States' capacity to provide quality early intervention services and expand and improve existing early intervention services being provided to infants and toddlers with handicaps and their families.

303.2 Eligible applicants for an award.

Eligible applicants include the 50 States, Puerto Rico, the District of Columbia, the Secretary of the Interior, and the following jurisdictions: Guam, American Samoa, the Virgin Islands, the Republic of Palau, and the Commonwealth of the Northern Mariana Islands.

303.3 Activities that may be supported under this part.

Funds under this part may be used for the following activities:

(a) To plan, develop, and implement a statewide system of early intervention services for infants and toddlers with handicaps and their families.

(b) To fund direct services that are not otherwise provided from other public or private sources.

(c) To expand and improve on services that are otherwise available.

303.4 Applicable regulations.

(a) The following regulations apply to this part:

(1) The Education Department General Administrative Regulations (EDGAR) in 34 CFR [Code of Federal Regulations] Part 74 (Administration of Grants), Part 76 (State-Administered Programs), Part 77 (Definitions That Apply to Department Regulations), Part 78 (Education Appeal Board), and Part 79 (Intergovernmental Review of Department of Education Programs and Activities).

(2) The regulations in this Part 303.

(3) The following regulations in 34 CFR Part 300 (Assistance to States for Education of Handicapped Children); 300.6; 300.9; 300.10; 300.12; 300.13(b)(1), (4), (5), (7), (8), (11), and (12); 300.500; and 300.581–300.586.

(b) In applying the regulations cited in paragraphs (a)(1) and (a)(3) of this section, any reference to –

(1) "State educational agency" means the lead agency under this part; and

(2) "Special education," "related services," "free public education," or "education" means early intervention services under this part.

Definitions

303.5 Act.

As used in this part, "Act" means the Education of the Handicapped Act.

303.6 Case management services.

(a) As used in this part, "case management services" means services provided to families of infants and toddlers with handicaps to assist them in gaining access to early intervention services identified in the individualized family service plan.

(b) Case management services include –

(1) Coordinating the performance of evaluations and participating in the development of the individualized family service plan;

(2) Assisting families in identifying available service providers;

(3) Coordinating and monitoring the delivery of services, including coordinating the provision of early intervention services with other services that the child or family needs or is being provided, but that are not required under this part (e.g., medical services for other than diagnostic or evaluation purposes, respite care, and the purchase of personal prosthetic devices such as braces, hearing aids, and glasses); and

(4) Facilitating the development of a transition plan to preschool services, where appropriate.

303.7 Child; children.

As used in this part, "child" and "children" mean "infants and toddlers with handicaps," as that term is defined in 303.13.

303.8 Council.

As used in this part, "Council" means the State Interagency Coordinating Council.

303.9 Developmental Delay.

As used in this part "developmental delay," has the meaning given to that term by a State under 303.60.

303.10 Early intervention services.

(a) General. As used in this part, "early intervention services" means services that –

(1) Are designed to meet the developmental needs of infants and toddlers with handicaps in one or more of the areas listed in 303.13(a);

(2) Are provided in conformity with an individualized family service plan;

(3) Are provided under public supervision;

(4) Meet the standards of the State, including the requirements of this part; and

(5) Are provided at no cost unless Federal or State law provides for a system of payments by families, including a schedule of sliding fees.

(b) Types of services. Early intervention services include –

(1) Audiology;

(2) Case managment services, as defined in 303.6;

(3) Early identification, screening, and assessment services;

(4) Family training, counseling, and home visits;

(5) Health services, as defined in 303.11;

(6) Medical services only for diagnostic and evaluation purposes;

(7) Occupational therapy;

(8) Physical therapy;

(9) Psychological services;

(10) Special instruction, as defined in 303.14; and

(11) Speech pathology.

(c) Qualified personnel. Early intervention services must be provided by qualified personnel, including —

(1) Audiologists;

(2) Nurses, including school nurses;

(3) Nutritionists;

(4) Occupational therapists;

(5) Physical therapists;

(6) Physicians;

(7) Psychologists, including school psychologists;

(8) Social workers, including school social workers;

(9) Special educators; and

(10) Speech and language pathologists.

Note: The lists of services and personnel in paragraphs (b) and (c) are not exhaustive and may include other types of services or personnel. Examples of other eligible services include transportation, rehabilitation technology, and music therapy.

303.11 Health services.

As used in this part, "health services" means services necessary to enable a child to benefit from other early intervention services (e.g., clean intermittent catheterization). The term does not include those services that are surgical or purely medical in nature (e.g., cleft palate surgery, surgery for club foot, management of cystic fibrosis, and shunting of hydrocephalus).

303.12 IFSP.

As used in this part, "IFSP" means the individualized family service plan.

303.13 Infants and toddlers with handicaps.

(a) As used in this part, "infants and toddlers with handicaps" means children from birth through age two who need early intervention services because they —

(1) Are experiencing developmental delays, as measured by appropriate diagnostic instruments and procedures, in one or more of the following areas: Cognitive development, physical development, language and speech development, psychosocial development, or self-help skills; or

(2) Have a diagnosed physical or mental condition that has a high probability of resulting in developmental delay.

(b) The term may also include, at a State's discretion, children from birth through two who are at risk of having substantial developmental delays if early intervention services are not provided.

Note: The phrase "have a diagnosed physical or mental condition that has a high probability of resulting in developmental delay" is included to enable States to serve categories of infants and toddlers who will need early intervention services, even though many may not exhibit developmental delays at the time of diagnosis (e.g., children with sensory impairments, inborn errors of metabolism, microcephaly, fetal alcohol syndrome. epilepsy and Down Syndrome and other chromosomal abnormalities).

303.14 Special instruction.

(a) As used in this part, "special instruction" means instruction provided to infants and toddlers and their families by special educators or other qualified personnel.

(b) Special instruction may be provided in the child's home, early intervention centers, hospitals and clinics, or other settings, as appropriate to the age and needs of the individual child.

Applicable Definitions in EDGAR and Part B of the Act

303.15 EDGAR definitions that apply.

The following terms used in this part are defined in 34 CFR 77.1:

Applicant	Grant
Award	Grantee
Contract	Grant period
Department	Private
EDGAR	Public
Equipment	Secretary
Fiscal year	State

303.16 Applicable definitions in the regulations for Part B of the Act.

The following terms used in this part are defined in 34 CFR Part 300, the regulations that implement Part B of the Education of the Handicapped Act. The section of Part 300 that contains the definition is given in parentheses.

Audiology (300.13(1))
Include (300.6)
Medical services (300.13(4))
Native language (300.9)
Occupational therapy (300.13(5))
Parent (300.10)
Personally identifiable information (300.500)
Physical therapy (300.13(7))
Psychological services (300.13(8))
Public agency (300.11)
Qualified (300.12)
Speech pathology (300.13(12))

Subpart B—State Application for a Grant

General Requirements

303.20 Conditions of assistance.

In order to receive funds under this part for any fiscal year, a State shall—

(a) Submit an annual application to the Secretary through the lead agency designated by the Governor; and

(b) Have on file with the Secretary the statement of assurances required under 303.23–303.30.

303.21 Public participation.

(a) General. (1) Before a State submits its annual application under this part, and before the adoption of policies in that application, the State shall provide –

      (i) Public hearings;

      (ii) Adequate notice of the hearings; and

      (iii) An opportunity for comment by the general public.

(2) As used in paragraph (a)(1) of this section, the term "policies" includes –

      (i) A State's definition of "developmental delay";

      (ii) A statement of what fees will be charged for early intervention services and the basis for those fees;

      (iii) A State's policy regarding the provision of services to children who are "at risk";

      (iv) The components of the statewide system; and

      (v) Other policies required to be included in the State application.

(b) Notice. The notice of public hearings must be published or announced –

(1) In newspapers or other media, or both, with coverage adequate to notify the general public throughout the State about the hearings;

(2) Sufficiently in advance of the date of the hearings to afford interested parties throughout the State a reasonable opportunity to participate; and

(3) In sufficient detail to inform the public about –

      (i) The purpose and scope of the State application and its relationship to Part H of the Act;

      (ii) The date, time, and location of each hearing; and

      (iii) The procedures for providing oral comments or submitting written comments.

303.22 How the Secretary disapproves a State's application or statement of assurances.

The Secretary follows the procedures in 34 CFR 300.580–300.586 before disapproving a State's application or statement of assurances submitted under this part.

Statement of Assurances

303.23 General.

A statement of assurances is a document that –

(a) Contains the information in 303.24–303.30;

(b) Is submitted only once and remains in effect throughout the term of a State's participation under this part; and

(c) Is filed with the Secretary at the time the State submits its application for the first year of assistance under this part.

303.24 Reports and records.

The statement must provide for —

(a) Making reports in such form and containing such information as the Secretary may require; and

(b) Keeping records and affording access to those records as the Secretary may find necessary to assure the correctness and verification of reports and of proper disbursement of funds provided under this part.

303.25 Control of funds and property.

The statement must provide assurance satisfactory to the Secretary that the control of funds provided under this part, and title to property acquired with those funds, is in a public agency for the uses and purposes provided in this part, and that a public agency administers the funds and property.

303.26 Prohibition against commingling.

The statement must include an assurance satisfactory to the Secretary that funds made available under this part will not be commingled with State funds.

303.27 Prohibition against supplanting.

The statement must include an assurance satisfactory to the Secretary that Federal funds made available under this part will be used to supplement and increase the level of State and local funds expended for infants and toddlers with handicaps and their families and in no case to supplant those State and local funds.

303.28 Fiscal control.

The statement must provide assurance satisfactory to the Secretary that such fiscal control and fund accounting procedures will be adopted as may be necessary to assure proper disbursement of, and accounting for, Federal funds paid under this part.

303.29 Assurance regarding nonsubstitution of funds.

The statement must include an assurance satisfactory to the Secretary that the State will comply with the requirements in 303.85(b).

303.30 Assurance regarding use of funds.

The statement must include an assurance satisfactory to the Secretary that the funds paid to the State under this part will be expended in accordance with the provisions of this part.

General Requirements for a State Application

303.31 General.

A State's annual application under this program must contain the information required in 303.32–303.27.

303.32 Information about State Interagency Coordinating Council.

Each application must include information demonstrating that the State has established a State Interagency Coordinating Council that meets the requirements of Subpart E.

303.33 Designation of lead agency.

Each application must include an assurance that funds received under this part will be used to assist the State to plan, develop, and implement the Statewide system required under 303.60–303.86.

303.15 Description of use of funds.

Each application must include the following information:

(a) For both the lead agency and the State Interagency Coordinating Council—

(1) A list of administrative positions, and a description of duties for each person whose salary is paid in whole or in part with funds awarded under this part; and

(2) For each position, the percentage of salary paid with those funds.

(b) A description of the nature and scope of the activities to be carried out with funds under this part during the period for which the award is to be made. The description must include information about—

(1) The Statewide planning, development, and implementation activities to be carried out by the Council, the lead agency, and any other agencies in the State that are involved in early intervention services;

(2) The approximate amount of funds that will be expended to carry out each activity described in paragraph (b)(1) of this section; and

(3) Any direct services that will be provided.

303.36 Information about public participation.

(a) Each application must include—

(1) Information demonstrating that the State has met the requirements on public participation under 303.21.

(2) A summary of the public comments received; and

(3) The State's responses to those comments.

(b) The information in paragraph (a)(1) of this section must include copies of news releases and advertisements used to provide notice, and a list of the dates and locations of the hearings.

303.37 Equitable distribution of resources.

Each application must include a description of the procedures used by the State to ensure an equitable distribution of resources made available under this part among all geographic areas within the State.

303.38 Application requirements for first and second years.

A State's annual application for the first and second years of participation under this program must contain the information required in 303.32–303.37.

303.39 Third year application.

A State's application for the third year of participation under this program must contain—

(a) The information required in 303.32–303.37;

(b) Information and assurances demonstrating that the State has adopted a policy that incorporates all of the components of a statewide system of early intervention services, as required in 303.60–303.86, or that the State has obtained a waiver from the Secretary; and

(c) Information and assurance satisfactory to the Secretary that the statewide system will be in effect no later than the beginning of the fourth year of participation, except that with respect to IFSPs, the State need only –

(1) Conduct multidisciplinary assessments;

(2) Develop IFSPs; and

(3) Make available case management services.

303.40 Waiver of the policy adoption requirement for the third year.

The Secretary may award a grant to a State under this part for the third year even if the State has not adopted the policy required in 303.39(b), if the State, in its application –

(a) Demonstrates that it has made a good faith effort to adopt such a policy;

(b) Provides the reasons why it was unable to meet the time line;

(c) Describes the steps remaining before the policy is adopted; and

(d) Provides an assurance that the policy will go into effect before the beginning of the fourth year of its participation under this part.

Note: An example of when the Secretary may grant a waiver is a situation in which a policy is awaiting action by the State legislature, but the legislative session does not commence until after the State's application must be submitted.

303.41 Fourth year applications.

A State's application for the fourth year of participation under this program must contain all of the information required by 303.39 (State application for the third year). However, in its application for the fourth year, the State may incorporate by reference any portions of its third year application that are still in effect.

303.42 States with mandates as of September 1, 1986, to serve children with handicaps from birth.

(a) Subject to the requirements of paragraph (b) of this section, a State that has in effect a State law, enacted before September 1, 1986, that requires the provision of a free appropriate public education to children with handicaps from birth through age two is eligible for a grant under this part for the first through the fourth year of its participation.

(b) A State meeting the conditions of paragraph (a) of this section must –

(1) Have on file with the Secretary a statement of assurances containing the information required in 303.24–303.30;

(2) Submit an annual application for years one through four that contains the information in 303.32–303.37;

(3) Meet the public participation requirements in 303.21; and

(4) Provide a copy of the State law that requires the provision of a free appropriate public education to children with handicaps from birth through age two.

(c) In order to receive funds under this part for the fifth and succeeding years, the State must submit an application that meets the requirements of 303.43.

Note: A State that qualifies under this section is exempted from submitting the information about the statewide system of early intervention services in 303.60–303.86 that is required in the applications for years three and four. However, in order to receive funds under this part for the fifth and succeeding years, the State must include in its application for those years information demonstrating that the statewide system is in effect.

303.43 Applications for year five and each year thereafter.

A State's annual applications for the fifth and succeeding years of participation under this program must contain –

(a) The information required in 303.32–303.37; and

(b) Information and assurances demonstrating to the satisfaction of the Secretary that the State has in effect the statewide system required in 303.60–303.86.

Participation by the Secretary of the Interior for Assistance

The Secretary of the Interior may receive an award under this part only after submitting an application that –

(a) Meets the conditions of assistance required by 303.20; and

(b) Is approved by the Secretary.

Subpart C – Procedures for Making Grants to States

303.50 Formula for State allocations.

(a) For each fiscal year, from the aggregate amount of funds available under this part for distribution to the States, the Secretary allots to each State an amount that bears the same ratio to the aggregate amount as the number of infants and toddlers in the State bears to the number of infants and toddlers in all States.

(b) For the purposes of allotting funds to the States under paragraph (a) of this section –

(1) "Aggregate amount" means the amount available for distribution to the States after the Secretary determines the amount of payments to be made to the Secretary of the Interior under 303.53 and to the jurisdictions under 303.54; and

(2) "State" means the 50 States, the District of Columbia, and the Commonwealth of Puerto Rico.

303.51 Distribution of allotments from nonparticipating States.

If a State elects not to receive its allotment, the Secretary may allot those funds among the remaining States in accordance with 303.50.

303.52 Minimum grant that a State may receive.

No State receives less than 0.5 percent of the aggregate amount available under 303.50.

303.53 Payments to the Secretary of the Interior.

(a) The Secretary is authorized to make payments to the Secretary of the Interior according to the need for assistance for the provision of early intervention services to children with handicaps and their families on reservations served by the elementary and secondary schools operated for Indians by the Department of the Interior.

(b) The amount of payment under paragraph (a) of this section for any fiscal year is 1.25 percent of the aggregate amount available to States after the Secretary determines the amount of payments to be made to the jurisdictions under 303.54.

303.54 Payments to the jurisdictions.

From the sums appropriated to carry out this part for any fiscal year, the Secretary may reserve up to 1 percent for payments to the jurisdictions listed in 303.2 in accordance with their respective needs.

Subpart D — Minimum Components of a Statewide System of Early Intervention Services

General Components

303.60 State definition of developmental delay.

Each State's policies must include the definition of the term "developmental delay" that will be used by the State in carrying out programs under this part. The State's definition must include the five developmental areas listed in 303.13.

303.61 Central directory.

(a) Each system must have a central directory, that includes information about —

(1) Early intervention services, resources, and experts available in the State; and

(2) Research and demonstration projects being conducted in the State.

(b) The central directory must be —

(1) Updated at least annually, and

(2) Easily accessible to the public.

Note: To the extent appropriate, the directory should include available parent support groups and advocate associations.

303.62 Timetables for serving all eligible children.

Each system must include timetables for ensuring that appropriate early intervention services will be available to all infants and toddlers with handicaps by the beginning of the fifth year of the State's participation under this part.

Identification and Evaluation

303.63 Public awareness program.

Each system must include a public awareness program that focuses on early identification services for infants and toddlers with handicaps. The program must—

(a) Be a continuous, ongoing program that is in effect throughout the State; and

(b) Provide for the involvement of, and communication with, major organizations throughout the State that have a direct interest in this part, including public agencies at the State and local level, private providers, parent groups, advocate associations, and other organizations.

303.64 Comprehensive child find system.

(a) Each system must include a comprehensive child find system that meets the requirements of paragraphs (b) through (d) of this section.

(b) The child find system must—

(1) Be consistent with the State's child identification, location, and evaluation procedures required under Part B of the Act (see 34 CFR 300.128);

(2) Be coordinated with all other major child find efforts conducted by various public and private agencies throughout the State; and

(3) Include procedures for making referrals by primary referral sources to the child find system and to service providers.

(c) The procedures in paragraph (b)(3) of this section must include—

(1) Reasonable time lines; and

(2) Provide for participation by primary referral sources, including hospitals and postnatal care facilities, physicians, parents, other health care providers, public health facilities, and day care programs.

Note 1: Coordination with other child find efforts in the State helps to maximize the State's resources by eliminating duplication of effort and ensuring that all eligible children are identified. To ensure appropriate coverage, a State may wish to establish a central registry.

Note 2: A State should establish reasonable time lines (e.g., 30 calendar days) for staff in the child find system to act on a referral (e.g., (1) in determining a child's eligibility after referral to the child find system, and (2) in referring the child to a service provider after the need for early intervention services has been determined). This will help ensure that delays in identification, evaluation, and the provision of services are minimal.

303.65 Evaluation and assessment.

(a) Each system must include the performance of a timely, comprehensive, multidisciplinary evaluation of each child, birth through age two, referred for evaluation. The evaluation must meet the requirements of paragraph (b) through (d) of this section.

(b) The evaluation required by paragraph (a) of this section must include the following:

(1) For each child —

(i) An evaluation or the child's level of functioning in all five areas listed in 303.13(a);

(ii) An assessment of the unique needs of the child; and

(iii) The identification of services appropriate to meet those needs.

(2) For the family of each child, an assessment of the family's strengths and needs relating to enhancing the development of the child.

(c) To the extent appropriate, the assessment of families in paragraph (b)(2) of this section must be based on information provided by the families through personal interviews or written statements.

(d) The evaluation and assessment of each child and the child's family must be completed within 30 calendar days after referral.

Note: Section 303.65 combines into one overall requirement the provisions on evaluation and assessment under the following sections of the Act: Section 676(b)(3) (timely, comprehensive, multidisciplinary evaluation), and section 677(a)(1) (multidisciplinary assessment). It also requires that the evaluation-assessment process be broad enough to include information required in the IFSP concerning (1) The family's strengths (section 677(d)(2)), and the child's functioning level in self-help skills and in physical, cognitive, speech-language, and psychosocial development (section 676(d)(1)).

The evaluation-assessment requirement in 303.65 may be completed as a one or two step process, depending upon State practice. However, the State: (1) Must ensure that the process is completed before writing the IFSP, and (2) should provide for appropriate participation by the families of the infants and toddlers.

Individualized Family Service Plan

303.66 Meeting the IFSP requirements.

(a) General. Each system must include procedures that meet the requirements of this section and 303.67–303.70.

(b) Requirements for the third year. Except as provided in 303.40, the procedures required in paragraph (a) of this section must be included in a State's third year application under this part.

(c) Fourth year requirements. By the beginning of the fourth year of a State's participation under this part, the State shall ensure that the following are met:

(1) The evaluation and assessment requirement in 303.65 is implemented.

(2) An IFSP is developed for each child determined to be eligible under this part. The IFSP must —

(i) Be developed by an interdisciplinary team, including the parents;

(ii) Be based on the results of the evaluation in 303.65; and

(iii) Be developed within a reasonable time after the multidisciplinary evaluation is completed.

(3) Case management services are available to the family of each child.

(d) Requirements for the fifth and succeeding years. By the beginning of the fifth year of a State's participation, an IFSP must be developed and implemented for each child who is eligible for early intervention services. *Note:* Development of the IFSP is essentially the final step in the evaluation-assessment process. Therefore, it is expected that the IFSP for a child who has been evaluated under 303.65 would be developed as soon as possible after the evaluation is completed (e.g., by the end of the 30-day time line in 303.65(d), or within a few days of that time line).

303.67 Provision of services before assessment is completed.

With parental consent, early intervention services may commence before the completion of the evaluation in 303.65. However, within 30 calendar days of the initiation of those services, the evaluation must be completed and the IFSP must be developed.

Note: The report of the House of Representatives on Pub. L. 99-457 includes the following statement regarding the provision of services before completing the evaluation of an infant or toddler:

The authority to allow early intervention services to commence prior to completion of assessment should be the exception and not the rule. Further, this authority should not be used as a means for systematically circumventing the obligation to complete the assessment and develop the plan within a reasonable time (House Report No. 99-860, 1986).

303.68 Review and evaluation of IFSP.

(a) Periodic review. Each child's IFSP must be evaluated once a year, and the family must be provided a review of the IFSP at 6-month intervals (or more often, if appropriate, based on the child's or family's needs).

(b) Family participation. The review and evaluation of each child's IFSP must provide for the participation of the child's family.

303.69 Content of IFSP.

The IFSP for each child must be in writing, and contain –

(a) A statement of the child's present levels of physical development, cognitive development, language and speech development, psychosocial development, and self-help skills, based on acceptable objective criteria;

(b) A statement of the family's strengths and needs relating to enhancing the development of the child;

(c) A statement of the major outcomes expected to be achieved for the child and the family, including the criteria, procedures, and time lines that will be used to determine –

(1) The degree to which progress toward achieving the outcomes is being made; and

(2) Whether modifications or revisions of the outcomes or services are necessary;

(d) A statement of the specific early intervention services necessary to meet the unique needs of the child and the family, including the frequency, intensity, and method of delivering services;

(e) The projected dates for initiation of services and the anticipated duration of those services;

(f) The name of the case manager from the profession most immediately relevant to the child's or family's needs, who will be responsible for the implementation of the IFSP and coordination with other agencies and persons; and

(g) The steps to be taken supporting the transition of the child to services provided under Part B of the Act, to the extent that those services are considered appropriate.

303.70 Responsibility and accountability.

Each agency or person who has a direct role in the provision of early intervention services is responsible for making a good faith effort to assist each eligible child in achieving the outcomes in the child's IFSP. However, Part H of the Act does not require that any agency or person be held accountable if an eligible child does not achieve the growth projected in the child's IFSP.

Personnel Training and Standards

303.71 Comprehensive system of personnel development.

(a) Each system must include a comprehensive system of personnel development. Subject to paragraph (b) of this section, a State's current personnel development system required under Part B of the Act (See 34 CFR 300.380–300.387) may be used to satisfy this requirement.

(b) The personnel development system under this part must—

(1) Provide for preservice and inservice training to be conducted on an interdisciplinary basis, to the extent appropriate; and

(2) Provide for the training of a variety of personnel needed to meet the requirements of this part, including public and private providers, primary referral sources, parents, paraprofessionals, and persons who will serve as case managers.

303.72 Standards for personnel who provide services to infants and toddlers with handicaps.

(a) General requirement. (1) Each system must include policies and procedures for establishing and maintaining standards to ensure that personnel necessary to provide early intervention services under this part are appropriately and adequately prepared and trained.

(2) The standards required by paragraph (a)(1) of this section must be consistent with any State approved or recognized certification, licensing, or other comparable requirements that apply to the profession or discipline in which personnel are providing early intervention services.

(b) Information. Each system must include a list that —

(1) Shows each profession or discipline in which personnel are providing early intervention services; and

(2) Indicates, for each profession or discipline, whether the applicable standards are consistent with the highest requirements in the State for that profession or discipline.

(c) Steps; time lines. For each area of early intervention services in which the existing State standards are not based on the highest requirements in the State applicable to a specific profession or discipline, the system must include —

(1) The steps the State is taking to require the retraining or hiring of personnel that meet the highest requirements in the State, and the time lines for accomplishing those steps; or

(2)(i) An alternative personnel standard that the State determines is appropriate;

(ii) A statement explaining the State's determination that this standard is appropriate;

(iii) The steps, if necessary, the State is taking to require the retraining or hiring of personnel that meet the State's alternative appropriate standards; and

(iv) The time lines for accomplishing those steps.

———————————

Authors' Note: The material in 303.72(c)(2)(i–iv) is not in the law. This is one example of how the administering agency, which writes the regulations, can attempt to alter the intent of the original legislation. At this writing, the regulations have not been finalized, so this matter could be dropped, altered, or retained in the final version of the regulations, depending to a large extent on the public comments received during the comment period.

———————————

(d) Highest requirements — all State agencies. In identifying the "highest requirements in the State" for purposes of this section, the requirements of all State agencies, not only the State educational agency, must be considered. *Note:* Identifying the "highest requirements in the State" means, for example, that if standards for physical therapists are issued by both the State educational agency (SEA) and a State licensing board, the standards of the SEA and the licensing board must be compared to identify the "highest requirements in the State."

Procedural Safeguards
303.73 General.

Each system must include procedural safeguards that meet the requirements in 303.74–303.82. A State may meet those requirements by —

(a) Adopting the full set of procedural safeguards in the regulations implementing Part B of the Act (See 34 CFR 300.500–300.514 and 300.560–300.576);

(b) Adopting selected parts of the procedural safeguards under Part B, and developing procedures to meet the remaining safeguards under 303.74–303.82; or

(c) Developing procedures that meet all the requirements under 303.74–303.82.

303.74 Opportunity to examine records.

The parents of a child covered under this part must be afforded the opportunity to examine records relating to assessment, screening, eligibility determinations, and the development and implementation of the IFSP.

303.75 Prior notice; native language.

(a) Written prior notice must be given to the parents of each child covered under this part a reasonable time before the State agency or service provider proposes, or refuses, to initiate or change the identification, evaluation, or placement of the child, or the provision of appropriate early intervention services to the child.

(b) The notice must —

    (1) Be in sufficient detail to fully inform the parents about —

        (i) The action that is being proposed or refused;

        (ii) The reasons for taking the action; and

        (iii) All procedural safeguards that are available under this part;

    (2) Be written in language understandable to the general public; and

    (3) Be provided in the native language of the parents unless it is clearly not feasible to do so.

303.76 Administrative complaint procedures.

Each system must include procedures for the timely administrative resolution of individual child complaints by parents concerning any of the matters listed in 303.75(a). The procedures must meet the requirements in 303.77–303.82.

Note: Regarding the timely resolution of complaints by parents. The Report of the House of Representatives on Pub. L. 99-457 states:

It is also the Committee's intent that the procedures developed by the State result in speedy resolution of complaints because an infant's development is rapid and therefore undue delay could be potentially harmful. Thus, it would be acceptable for the impartial individual to attempt to mediate the complaint. However, if such an attempt is unsuccessful, it would be expected that the record be retained and that the decision be in writing to allow a parent, who is so inclined, to appeal to the courts. (House Report No. 99-860, 1986)

303.77 Appointment of an impartial person.

(a) Qualifications and duties. An impartial person must be appointed to implement the complaint resolution process. The person must —

(1) Have knowledge about the provisions of this part, and the needs and services available for, infants and toddlers with handicaps; and

(2) Perform the following duties:

(i) Listen to presentations of relevant viewpoints about the complaint, examine all information relevant to the issues, and seek to reach a timely resolution of the complaint; and

(ii) Provide a record of the proceedings, including a written decision.

(b) Definition of impartial. (1) As used in this section, "impartial" means that the person appointed to implement the complaint resolution process—

(i) Is not an employee of any agency involved in providing early intervention services to the child involved in the complaint; and

(ii) Does not have a personal or professional interest that would conflict with his or her objectivity in implementing the process.

(2) A person who otherwise qualifies to conduct a hearing under paragraph (b)(1) of this section is not an employee of an agency solely because he or she is paid by the agency to implement the complaint resolution process.

303.78 Convenience of proceedings; time lines.

(a) The administrative proceedings required under this part must be carried out at a time and place that is reasonably convenient to the parents.

(b) The State shall ensure that not later than 30 calendar days after receipt of a parent's complaint the administrative proceedings will be completed and a written decision mailed to each of the parties.

303.79 Civil action.

Any party aggrieved by the findings and decision regarding an administrative complaint has the right to bring a civil action in State or Federal court under section 680(1) of the Act.

303.80 Status of child during proceedings.

(a) During the pendency of any proceeding or action involving a complaint, unless the State agency and parents of a child otherwise agree, the child must continue to receive the appropriate early intervention services currently being provided.

(b) If the complaint involves an application for initial services under this part, the child must receive those services that are not in dispute.

303.81 Surrogate parents.

Each system must include procedures to protect the rights of a child covered under this part whenever the parents of the child are unknown or unavailable, or the child is a ward of the State. The procedures must provide for the assignment of an individual to act as a surrogate for the parents. The person selected to serve as a surrogate parent may not be an employee of a State agency providing services to the child.

303.82 Confidentiality of information.

Each State shall adopt or develop policies and procedures that the State will follow in order to ensure the protection of any personally identifiable information collected, used, or maintained under this part.

303.83 Lead agency.

(a) General. Each statewide system must include a single line of responsibility in a lead agency that —

(1) Is established or designated by the Governor; and

(2) Is responsible for the administration of the system.

(b) Administrative duties. The lead agency is responsible for carrying out the following duties:

(1) General administration, supervision, and monitoring of programs and activities receiving assistance under this part to ensure compliance with the provisions of this part.

(2) Identification and coordination of all available resources within the State from Federal, State, local, and private sources.

(3) Assignment of financial responsibility to the appropriate agency.

(4) Entry into formal interagency agreements that (consistent with State law) —

(i) Define the financial responsibility of each agency for paying for early intervention services;

(ii) Include procedures for resolving disputes; and

(iii) Include all additional components necessary to ensure meaningful cooperation and coordination.

(5) Development of procedures to ensure that services are provided to infants and toddlers with handicaps and their families in a timely manner, pending the resolution of disputes among public agencies or service providers.

(6) Resolution of intra-agency and interagency disputes.

Note: The Report of the House of Representatives on Pub. L. 99-457 states the following regarding the single line of responsibility in a lead agency:

Without this critical requirement, there is an abdication of responsibility for the provision of early intervention services for handicapped infants and toddlers. Although the bill recognizes the importance of interagency responsibility for providing or paying for appropriate services, it is essential that ultimate responsibility remain in a lead agency so that buck-passing among State agencies does not occur to the detriment of the handicapped infant or toddler.

303.84 Policy for arranging for services.

Each system must include a policy pertaining to contracting or making other arrangements with service providers to provide early intervention services, consistent with the provisions of this part. The policy must set out the conditions that the lead agency expects to be met by a service provider, including —

(a) The contents of the application to be used, if the lead agency elects to have providers apply for funds;

(b) The conditions of the contract to be used, if services are to be provided on a contract basis; or

(c) The requirements to be met, if other arrangements are used.

303.85 Timely reimbursement; nonsubstitution.

(a) Reimbursement procedure. Each system must include a procedure for securing the timely reimbursement of funds used under this part, in accordance with paragraph (b) of this section.

(b) Nonsubstitution of funds. Funds provided under this part may not be used to satisfy a financial commitment for services that would have been paid for from another public or private source but for the enactment of Part H of the Act. However, if it is considered necessary to prevent a delay in the timely provision of services to an eligible child or family, funds under this part may be used to pay the provider of services, pending reimbursement from the agency which has ultimate responsibility for the payment.

(c) Nonreduction of other benefits. Nothing in this part may be construed to reduce medical or other assistance available or to alter eligibility under Title V of the Social Security Act (relating to maternal and child health) or Title XIX of the Social Security Act (relating to Medicaid for infants and toddlers) within the State.

303.86 Data collection.

(a) General. Each system must include the procedures that the State uses to compile descriptive data on the statewide system. The procedures must meet the requirements of paragraphs (b) and (c) of this section.

(b) Process for collecting data. The procedures must include a process for —

(1) Collecting data from various agencies and service providers in the State;

(2) Making use of appropriate sampling methods if sampling is permitted; and

(3) Describing the sampling methods used if reporting to the Secretary.

(c) Kinds of data to be reported. The procedures must provide for reporting the following kinds of data:

(1) The numbers of eligible children and their families in the State who are in need of early intervention services (which may be based on a sampling of data).

(2) The numbers of eligible children and their families who are served.

(3) The types of services provided (which may be based on a sampling of data).

(4) Other information required by the Secretary, including information required under section 618 of the Act.

Subpart E – State Interagency Coordinating Council

303.90 Establishment of Council.

(a) A State that desires to receive financial assistance under this part shall establish a State Interagency Coordinating Council composed of 15 members.

(b) The Council and the chairperson of the Council must be appointed by the Governor. The Governor shall ensure that the membership of the Council reasonably represents the population of the State.

303.91 Composition.

The Council must be composed of the following:

(a) At least —

(1) Three members who are parents of infants and toddlers with handicaps or of handicapped children aged three through six;

(2) Three public or private providers of early intervention services;

(3) One representative from the State legislature;

(4) One person in personnel preparation.

(b) Other members representing each of the appropriate agencies involved in the provision of or payment for early intervention services to eligible children under this part, and others selected by the Governor.

Note: The Council should include a representative of the State educational agency who is responsible for, or knowledgeable about, the Pre-school Grants program under section 619 of the Act (34 CFR Part 301). Inclusion of such a person will help to ensure the smooth transition of any infants or toddlers who will require special education and related services under that program.

303.92 Meetings.

The Council must meet at least quarterly and in such places as it deems necessary. The meetings must be publicly announced, and, to the extent appropriate, be open and accessible to the general public.

303.93 Functions of Council.

The Council must —

(a) Advise and assist the lead agency in the performance of its administrative duties in 303.83(b), particularly in the —

(1) Identification of the sources of fiscal and other support for services for early intervention programs;

(2) Assignment of financial responsibility to the appropriate agency; and

(3) Promotion of the interagency agreements;

(b) Advise and assist the lead agency in the preparation of annual applications under this part, and amendments to those applications; and

(c) Prepare and submit an annual report to the Governor and to the Secretary on the status of early intervention programs operated within the State for infants and toddlers with handicaps and their families.

303.94 Conflict of interest.

No member of the Council may cast a vote on any matter that would provide direct financial benefit to that member or otherwise give the appearance of a conflict of interest.

303.95 Use of existing councils.

If a State established a Council before September 1, 1986, that is comparable to the requirements for a Council in 303.90–303.94, that Council is considered to be in compliance with those requirements. However, within four years after the date that a State accepts funds under this part, the State shall establish Council that complies in full with 303.90–303.94.

3

The Statewide Early Intervention System

Public Law 99-457 provides financial assistance and guidelines to states to help them plan, develop, and implement a statewide, comprehensive, coordinated, multidisciplinary, interagency program of early intervention services for handicapped infants and toddlers and their families. This new law does not require the creation of an entirely new array of services; instead, it provides financial assistance to help states coordinate the services that are available within each state into one accessible system. Where needed services are absent, the state is expected to develop them. Where the level of service is inadequate, the state would be expected to expand these services. With few exceptions, the services that will be required are already present in some form in the states.

There are numerous social programs already operating in each of the states that provide a variety of services for infants and toddlers and their families. These programs are funded by federal, state, and local governments, nonprofit agencies, and other private sources. Garwood, Phillips, Hartman, and Zigler (1989) have identified 93 programs operated by 13 federal agencies that provide a variety of services to America's children and their families. Collectively, these federal agency programs expended an estimated $118 billion during fiscal year 1986, and because many of these programs include a state match requirement, the amount actually expended on children and families is higher than $118 billion.

The 93 programs identified by Garwood et al. (1989) include Foster Grandparents (which provides services to children who are mentally retarded); Food Stamps; the Indian Health Program; Military Health Care Services; Chapter 1; Education of the Handicapped Act; Child Abuse Grants; Developmental Disabilities Program; Head Start; Alcohol, Drug Abuse, and Mental Health Block Grant; Aid to Families with Dependent Children; Maternal and Child Health Services Block Grant; Medicaid; and many others. Many of these programs provide services that are appropriate for incorporation into an early intervention system.

Early Intervention Services Available
in a Typical State

As an example of the present availability of some early intervention services, let's examine the variety and range of programs or activities for handicapped infants and toddlers that exist in one state. In South Carolina, a number of different agencies provide services to handicapped infants and toddlers and their families. These agencies include:

South Carolina Commission for the Blind
Offers a variety of services for blind children from birth to about age 16.

Charles Webb Easter Seal Center
Operates a center-based child development program for physically, mentally, and visually handicapped children under the age of 5.

Epworth Children's Home (a church-related agency)
Offers a center-based infant stimulation and parent training program for children from birth through 4, and a home-based early intervention program for medically at-risk infants, birth to 2.

South Carolina State Department of Education
Operates an interagency referral system for children from birth to age 21.

South Carolina Department of Health and Environmental Control
(the designated lead agency for Part H) Operates a variety of health-related programs through its county health offices, including prenatal clinics; WIC clinics; the High Risk Perinatal Program; child health clinics; Early Periodic Screening, Diagnosis, and Treatment clinics; and screening for lead toxicity, PKU, hypothyroidism, and sickle cell disease; tracks at-risk newborns; diagnoses and treats handicapping conditions; provides case coordination for eligible SSI recipients.

South Carolina Department of Mental Health
Offers outpatient diagnostic and treatment services, preventive services, emergency services, referral services, and consultation services for children under 6 and their families. Provides services to children with autism and their families, including early intervention services for children from birth to 5, parent support, and respite care.

South Carolina Department of Mental Retardation
For eligible children ages birth through 5, offers case management services, family support services, respite care, home-based early intervention services, diagnostic and evaluation services, genetic services, and center-based child development programs. Provides support for 47 community-based early intervention programs.

South Carolina Department of Social Services

Provides services to protect children and help maintain families, including case management.

Medical University of South Carolina

Operates newborn developmental follow-up clinics to assess the developmental progress of all high-risk infants who had been in neonatal intensive care units in the state, and refers these infants to appropriate follow-up services. Operates an early intervention program for selected high-risk infants beginning at 3 months of age.

South Carolina School for the Deaf and Blind

Operates a home-based parent/infant program for babies who are deafblind or multihandicapped sensory impaired.

Winthrop College Human Development Center

Provides evaluation and treatment services, including developmental therapy and early childhood education services.

South Carolina Center of Excellence in Early Childhood

Conducts research and training activities in early childhood special education.

University of South Carolina Center for Developmental Disabilities

Operates an interdisciplinary diagnostic clinic, parent support groups, training workshops, and case coordination services.

South Carolina Handicapped Services Information System

Provides a computerized information and referral system for early intervention services in the state; it is accessed by a toll-free telephone number.

The range of services offered by these South Carolina agencies includes screening, assessment and evaluation; center- and home-based early intervention programs for infants and toddlers with handicaps; early intervention support services; family counseling; case management; parent training; maternal and child health services; follow-up services for at-risk low birth weight infants; nutritional assessment; nutrition education; provision of prescribed supplemental foods to women, infants, and young children; genetic screening; screening for lead toxicity; psychotherapy for children and their families; individual psychotherapy; and in-home and out-of-home respite care.

In addition to the services noted above, various state agencies offer services that would help parents of handicapped children, including education, job training, child care assistance, and employment assistance. The type and quantity of these services and those enumerated in the previous paragraph vary somewhat throughout geographic areas of the state of South Carolina.

Despite the present availability of numerous services in this typical state, many of these early intervention services are not available to all who might need them. Agencies providing the service have differing eligibility criteria. Services offered by one agency are not coordinated with services offered by other agencies, and families are expected to gain access to many of these services on their own. It is the intent of P.L. 99-457 to encourage the organization of these separate services, available through separate agencies, into a comprehensive statewide system of early intervention services.

Responsibilities of the Lead Agency

Public Law 99-457 requires the governor of each state to designate one agency within the state to serve as the lead agency for developing and implementing the state's early intervention system. Table 3.1 contains a listing of the 14 minimum components required to be a part of this system. This lead state agency is responsible for identifying all available early intervention and family needs resources available in the state, and linking all these various services and programs into one statewide early intervention system. The lead agency is also responsible for managing the linkup of this early intervention system once it is in place, and this responsibility includes data collection on, and monitoring of, the early intervention services and programs that are part of the statewide system. In addition, the lead agency is also expected to identify services that need to be improved or expanded as well as services that might need to be developed.

Each state's lead agency is responsible for assigning financial responsibility for various early intervention services to the various agencies within the state that provide services. The lead agency also establishes interagency cooperative agreements with these other agencies so that all needed services will become available in a timely manner to an eligible infant or toddler and the family once a determination of these services is made by the team preparing the Individualized Family Service Plan (IFSP). Because it is likely that there may be disputes among agencies as to who should bear the cost of an early intervention service, the lead agency is also responsible for developing procedures to resolve such disputes. In developing these various procedures and policies governing the operation of the state's early intervention system, the lead agency should seek advice and assistance from the state's Interagency Coordinating Council, established under P.L. 99-457.

A state's lead agency is responsible for submitting the annual application for federal funds to the Secretary of Education. This application must identify the designated lead agency and must give assurances that the Interagency Coordinating Council has been established and that other eligibility criteria have been met. This application must also contain information about the public hearings held to gain citizen input into the development of the statewide early intervention system, and it must describe how the state intends to use

TABLE 3.1
Minimum Components of a Statewide Early Intervention System
(Part H, P.L. 99-457)

A. Designation of a lead agency with a single line of authority to carry out the administration of the program

B. Determination of a definition of "developmentally delayed"

C. Establishment of timetables to ensure full service to all eligible infants and toddlers and their families by year 5

D. Development of procedures to ensure the provision of timely, comprehensive, multidisciplinary evaluations of the functioning of eligible infants and toddlers, and the needs and strengths of the family

E. Development of an IFSP and provision of case management

F. Establishment of a comprehensive child-find system

G. Development of a public awareness program

H. Creation of a central directory of resources, experts, and research and demonstration projects in the state

I. Development of a comprehensive system of personnel preparation

J. Development of a policy governing contractual arrangements with local service providers

K. Establishment of acceptable due process procedures

L. Enactment of a state policy that incorporates all components of the statewide early intervention system described in P.L. 99-457

M. Development of procedures for securing timely reimbursement of Part H funds

N. Establishment of a comprehensive early intervention data collection system

the federal funds provided under P.L. 99-457. In addition, the application must show that the early intervention funds will be equitably distributed across all geographic regions within the state.

Early Intervention Services Criteria

In organizing its array of early intervention services to form the state's comprehensive system, the lead agency must ensure that seven criteria are met. Table 3.2 lists these seven criteria.

TABLE 3.2
Early Intervention Services Criteria
(Part H, P.L. 99-457)

1. Services must be provided under public supervision; the ultimate responsibility remains with the lead agency.

2. Services must be provided at no costs except where federal or state law provides for payments, including a schedule of sliding fees.

3. Services must be designed to meet the child's developmental needs across at least five behavior domains.

4. Services must meet the standards of the state (refers to licensing, credentialing, and other standards established by the state for operation of facilities, use of qualified personnel, etc.).

5. Services must include a variety of options, including assessment, family training, counseling, home visits, special instruction, speech and audiology, physical therapy, case management, psychological services, and limited medical services.

6. Services must be provided by qualified personnel.

7. Services must be provided in conformity with an IFSP.

Time Lines for Developing an Early Intervention System

The law specifies time lines that must be met by a state as it moves to create its statewide early intervention system.

Years 1 and 2. During the first 2 years of its participation, a state may use its P.L. 99-457 funds to plan, develop, and implement its statewide early intervention system. In addition, during this time a state can use these funds to support the provision of direct services to infants and toddlers with handicaps if such services are not provided by other public or private sources, and the state can use these funds to expand and improve existing services. Thus, during these first 2 years, states are expected to be involved in such activities as (a) developing their definition of developmental delay; (b) reaching the decision regarding service to at-risk populations; (c) developing child-find and public awareness procedures; (d) determining what services are available; (e) establishing collaborative interagency agreements for providing and paying for early intervention services; and (f) developing policies governing such issues as family assessment and development of the individualized family service plan, provision of case management services, and local service provider contractual arrangements.

Years 3 and 4. During the third and fourth years of their participation, states are expected to continue their planning, development, implementation, and, where appropriate, service delivery or expansion activities. During the third year a state is required to adopt a policy incorporating all of the specified 14 components of a statewide, comprehensive early intervention system as specified in P.L. 99-457. Such a policy might include a restatement of all the components specified in P.L. 99-457, or it could be a brief statement that incorporates all 14 components by reference to the required provisions in P.L. 99-457.

It is this adoption of an early intervention policy that is critical to the success of P.L. 99-457, because such a policy signifies a long-term commitment by the state to the operation of the early intervention system described in the law. This policy, to be effective, will likely reflect a decision by a state's legislature, and will not be just a governor's executive order or a lead agency decision. The enactment of such a policy is a commitment of a state's fiscal resources, and it must have state legislative power behind it to ensure that all relevant agencies participate in the service delivery aspects and the cost-sharing aspects of a statewide, comprehensive early intervention system.

Public Law 99-457 does allow the Secretary of Education to grant a one-time waiver of the requirement that a state adopt a policy incorporating all the components of the early intervention system. Should such a waiver be granted, the state would be expected to have adopted *and implemented* such a policy before the beginning of a state's fourth year of financial assistance under P.L. 99-457.

Limited Implementation. Public Law 99-457 requires that the statewide early intervention system that the state has been involved in planning and developing for at least 3 years be partially implemented by the beginning of the fourth year of a state's participation. More specifically, the law requires that during the fourth year, a state only has to (a) conduct multidisciplinary assessments of infants and toddlers and their families; (b) develop individualized family service plans; and (c) provide case management services. These components are discussed in more detail below.

Year 5 and Thereafter. Beginning with the fifth year of participation, a state must have the complete early intervention system in operation in order to continue receiving federal funds under P.L. 99-457. Consequently, since all states have been participating in developing this early intervention system since fiscal year 1987, the fifth year for all states would be fiscal year 1991, which begins on October 1, 1991.

Definition of Developmental Delay

Public Law 99-457 does not define developmental delay; it leaves this determination up to each state to define as it wishes, consistent with the intent of the law. Because the law requires participating states to serve infants and toddlers who are delayed (in addition to serving those with a diagnosed condition that will likely lead to delay), the task for each state is to determine how much delay is necessary to establish eligibility for services.

States have several options. They can utilize "standard deviation cutoffs": That is, delay would be defined in terms of a standard deviation value below the norm for a child. For example, a child would be eligible if that child scored at least 1.5 standard deviation unit below the norm on one assessed domain or at least 1.0 standard deviation unit below the norm on two or more of the assessed behavioral domains. Similarly, states could use a "delay in months" criteria: An infant could be eligible, for example, if the infant is delayed by 3 months during the first year of life or by 6 months during the second year of life. Again, if the delay is present in more than one behavioral domain, the criteria would likely differ. A state might determine eligibility on the basis of 2 months delay in two or more assessed domains during the first year of life.

States could also use "percentages" to determine eligibility. If an infant is more than 25% delayed in one domain or more than 20% delayed in two or more domains, the infant would be deemed eligible for early intervention services. And, of course, states could use some combination of all three approaches. The values used in these examples are for illustrative purposes only. States must determine their own cut-off values, based on their own population figures and their available early intervention resources. Criteria being considered by various states for defining developmental delay include consideration of some combination of the following cut-off levels:

- 25% delay in one or more developmental areas;

- 1.5 standard deviations in at least one area;

- 6 months delay in two or more areas of development;

- severe, profound delay or severe sensory impairment or moderate delay or moderate sensory impairment, or substantial likelihood of becoming delayed;

- 2 standard deviations and/or a delay in months as follows:
  1 year of age: 3 months delay
  1.5 years of age: 4.5 months delay
  2 years of age: 6 months delay
  3 years of age: 9 months delay;

- 20% delay in at least one area of development;

- 1 standard deviation in two or more areas;

- 15% below chronological age in two or more areas of development:

- 25% below chronological age in two or more areas; 50% below chronological age in one area of development; and

- 40% below chronological age in one area of development (information provided through correspondence with the states).

In Chapter 4 we discuss these approaches in more detail.

States may also elect to serve at-risk infants and toddlers. Currently, states are deciding on the range of at-risk groups they wish to serve, and Table 3.3 contains a listing of the groups that have been identified by some states as potential at-risk groups. Of course, no state has indicated that it would serve all the groups identified in Table 3.3, only some small number of the groups contained in this table.

TABLE 3.3
Examples of Types of At-Risk Groups Under Consideration for Receipt of Early Intervention Services by the States

Children of Parents with Disability or Health Problems
Children of Substance Abuse Parents
Children Who Are Abused
Siblings of Abuse Victims
Children with Seriously Disturbed Parent/Child Relationships
Children in Highly Disruptive Families
Children of Teenage Parents
Children of Parents Over Age 35
Children of Low Income Parents
Children of Parents Without High School Educations
Siblings of an Identified Delayed Child
Infants Who Are Low Birth Weight or Premature
Children of Parents Lacking Prenatal Care
Children with Childhood Illnesses
Children of Parents Who Lack Access to Services
Children Who Lack Routine Well-Baby Care
Children of Parents Who Lack Support Systems
Children with Medical Conditions that Could Result in Delay
Children of Mothers Exposed to Medications Known to Cause Developmental Risk
Children with Inadequate Home Physical Environment
Children Who, at Age 3, Would Be Identified as Developmentally Disabled Under P.L. 94-142

Multidisciplinary Assessments

Public Law 99-457 requires that a comprehensive early intervention system include a multidisciplinary evaluation of the functioning of each eligible infant or toddler. More specifically, eligible infants and toddlers are to be assessed across at least five behavioral domains: physical, cognitive, language and speech, psychosocial, and self-help. The instruments or procedures that are used for this assessment must be appropriate and objective, and may be administered by various personnel involved in evaluating the behavioral capabilites of infants and toddlers.

Comprehensive infant assessment is important because it enables us to determine the presence and extent of both normally developing and atypically developing behaviors in the infant or toddler. This is information that is certainly useful in making decisions about placement of the child in an appropriate early intervention activity. Comprehensive infant assessment also provides us with a means for determining how the infant or toddler interacts with others and with the environment. This information provides helpful knowledge about child development, but also it provides the interventionist with clues about how to involve other people or the environment in intervention activities.

To successfully assess infant behavior requires knowledge not only of infant and toddler development but also of appropriate assessment instruments, their strengths and weaknesses. As Fewell (1983) has pointed out, "examiners must understand the impact of impairments on development, identify the behaviors to be assessed, select the multivariate procedures that will produce systematic evaluation, and then interpret the results in ways that can be translated easily into intervention programs" (p. 257).

Resources for Infant Development and Assessment

For the reader who wants to know more about infant development and infant assessment, we have included a list of resources that may prove helpful. This list is certainly not intended to be exhaustive, and a search of any nearby library will certainly reveal additional references that could be added to this list of resources.

Infant Development

Brazelton, T. B., & Yogman, M. W. (Eds.). (1986). *Affective development in infancy.* Norwood, NJ: Ablex.

Browman, S., Nichols, P. L., Shaughnessy, P., & Kennedy, W. (1987). *Retardation in young children.* Hillsdale, NJ: Erlbaum.

Cratty, B. J. (1986). *Perceptual and motor development in infants and children* (3rd ed.). Englewood Cliffs, NJ: Prentice-Hall.

Garwood, S. G., & Fewell, R. R. (Eds.). (1983). *Educating handicapped infants: Issues in development and intervention.* Rockville, MD: Aspen Systems.

Greenspan, S. (Ed.). (1987). *Infants in multirisk families: Case studies in prevention.* New York: International Universities Press.

Hanson, M. J. (Ed.). (1984). *Atypical infant development.* Austin, TX: PRO-ED.

Nelms, B. C., & Mullins, R. G. (1982). *Growth and development: A primary health care approach.* Englewood Cliffs, NJ: Prentice-Hall.

Osofsky, J. D. (Ed.). (1987). *Handbook of infant development* (2nd ed.). New York: Wiley.

Powell, G. J. (Ed.). (1983). *The psychosocial development of minority group children.* New York: Bruner/Mazel.

Rutter, M. (Ed.). (1983). *Developmental neuropsychiatry.* New York: Guilford.

Smith, M. J., Goodman, J. A., Ramsey, N. L., & Pasternack, S. B. (1982). *Child and family: Concepts of nursing practice.* New York: McGraw-Hill.

Trad, P. V. (1986). *Infant depression: Paradigms and paradoxes.* New York: Springer-Verlag.

Wachs, T., & Sheehan, R. (Eds.). (1988). *Assessment of developmentally disabled children.* New York: Plenum.

Wolff, P. H. (1987). *The development of behavioral states and the expression of emotions in infancy: New proposals for investigation.* Chicago: University of Chicago Press.

Infant Assessment

Brazelton, T. B. (1984). *Neonatal behavioral assessment scale* (2nd ed.). Philadelphia: J. B. Lippincott.

Fewell, R. R. (1983). *Assessing handicapped infants.* In S. G. Garwood & R. R. Fewell (Eds.), *Educating handicapped infants. Issues in development and intervention.* Rockville, MD: Aspen Systems.

Frankenburg, W. K., Emde, R. N., & Sullivan, J. W. (Eds.). (1985). *Early identification of children at risk: An international perspective.* New York: Plenum.

Kearsley, R. B., & Sigel, I. E. (Eds.). (1979). *Infants at risk: Assessment of cognitive functioning.* Hillsdale, NJ: Erlbaum.

Magrab, P. R. (Ed.). (1984). *Psychological and behavioral assessment: Impact on pediatric care.* New York: Plenum.

Rossetti, L. M. (1986). *High risk infants: Identification, assessment and intervention.* San Diego: College-Hill.

Stackj, J. M. (Ed.). (1982). *The special infant: An interdisciplinary approach to optimal development in infants.* New York: Human Services Press.

Ulrey, G., & Rogers, S. J. (1982). *Psychological assessment of handicapped infants and young children.* New York: Thieme-Stratton.

Uzgiris, I. C., & Hunt, J. McV. (Eds.). (1987). *Infant performance and experience: New findings with the ordinal scale.* Urbana: University of Illinois Press.

Van Hasselt, V. B., & Hersen, M. (1987). *Psychological evaluation of the developmentally and physically disabled.* New York: Plenum.

Family Needs and Strengths

The multidisciplinary assessment must also determine the strengths of the
infant's or toddler's family and their needs. Both of these areas of assessment
relate to the ability of the family to be effectively involved in efforts to intervene with their children.

The term *family needs* is not clarified in the law, but in general, it refers
to a process of identifying and satisfying needs of family members so that
they may more fully participate in the intervention activities of their child.
Needs could refer to such things as information about how to correctly position the child, how to recognize when the infant is responding, or knowledge
about typical developmental milestones in young children. But *needs* could
also refer to the need of the infant's mother to have time away from the
child (respite care), the family's need for brief therapy to recover from the
stress caused by the birth of a handicapped infant, or the need for more
long-term therapy for a mother who is depressed. Finally, *needs* could refer
to the need for job training, completion of a high school education, information about the availability of child care funding, or employment placement.
Any and all of these different types of needs could affect the success of
attempts to intervene effectively with an infant or toddler who is at risk for
delay, developmentally delayed, or handicapped.

The term *family strengths* refers to the identification of individual or family
resources that can be used in the intervention process with the family's infant.
Congress was careful to call for an assessment only of family strengths; however, it should be obvious that, in seeking to determine a strength, some
information about the absence of a strength is obtained.

Characteristics of a Strong Family.   Two large-scale studies of family
strengths have been done, and these may provide some clues as to what
is involved in determining family strengths. Stinnett, Chesser, and DeFrain
(1979) studied families who were identified as strong families, and they have
defined six common characteristics of strong families:

1. *Appreciation:* Members of strong families regarded each other warmly,
   positively, and gave support to each other as individuals.

2. *Time Together:* Members of strong families enjoyed spending time with
   family members.

3. *Good Communication Patterns:* Strong family members were honest, open,
   and receptive to other family members.

4. *Commitment:* To strong families, the family unit was important, as were
   the interpersonal subsystems within the family. Family members directed
   much energy and time inward toward the family.

5. *High Degree of Religious Orientation:* Strong families were anchored in a sense of purpose, which was often based in religious values. They possessed a spiritual sense that gave family members a common belief and promoted family values.

6. *Ability to Deal with Others:* Members of strong families were able to deal with conflicts, and they banded together in mutual support when bad times came about.

In a study of urban southern middle class families, Lewis, Beavers, Gossett, and Phillips (1976) found the following eight characteristics of optimal families:

1. an affiliative, not oppositional, attitude toward people;

2. respect for the subjective world view of others;

3. openness in communication as opposed to confusing/distancing communication patterns;

4. a firm, solid parental coalition in dealing with children, as opposed to parental competition;

5. appreciation for complex human motivation, as opposed to a simple controlling outlook;

6. spontaneity, as opposed to a rigid or stereotyped approach to interaction with others;

7. encouragement of the unique and creative in individuals, as opposed to encouragement of routine or bland human characteristics and interests;

8. a family organization that is a flexible and balanced structure as opposed to a rigid and conforming one.

In addition to the characteristics derived from the two studies cited above, Leventhal and Sabbeth (1986) have identified a number of factors that influence how a family cares for an ill child. For our purposes, these factors have been adapted to reflect the types of issues that assessors might want to consider when developing an approach to the assessment of the family. This adapted list would include:

Child Characteristics
- age and sex
- physical, cognitive, speech/language, and social development
- personality attributes
- temperament

- ability to care for self
- ability to form relations
- interaction characteristics with others
- interest in the environment and ability to interact with the environment

Parental Characteristics

As Individuals
- their own nurturing
- previous experience with stress
- importance of religion
- medical and psychiatric problems
- "success" in their own lives

As Parents
- relations with child
- relations with spouse and other significant adults
- meaning of the "handicap" to the parents

Family

- structure
- marital relations
- other relations
- financial resources
- support systems
- communication patterns
- power relationships

Social Setting and Cultural Context

- degree of poverty
- availability of health services
- availability of early intervention services
- availability of other needed services
- attitudes toward a handicap or disability

In addition to the resources cited above, the reader may find the following resources on families helpful.

The Family

Belsky, J., Lerner, R. M., & Spanier, G. B. (1984). *The child in the family*. Reading, MA: Addison-Wesley.

Darling, R. B., & Darling, J. (1982). *Children who are different: Meeting the challenges of birth defects in society*. St Louis: Mosby.

Feldman, R. A., Stiffman, A. R., & Jung, K. G. (1987). *Children at risk: In the web of parental mental illness*. New Brunswick, NJ: Rutgers University Press.

Garbarino, J. (1982). *Children and families in the social environment*. New York: Aldine.

Glendinning, C. (1983). *Unshared care: Parents and their disabled children*. London: Routledge.

Handleman, J. S., & Harris, S. L. (1986). *Educating the developmentally disabled: Meeting the needs of children and families*. San Diego: College-Hill.

Miezio, P. M. (1983). *Parenting children with disabilities: A professional source for physicians and guide for parents*. New York: Dekker.

Mori, A. (1983). *Families of children with special needs: Early intervention techniques for the practitioner*. Rockville, MD: Aspen Systems.

Moroney, R. (1986). *Shared responsibility: Family and social policy*. New York: Aldine.

Parke, R. D. (Ed.). (1984). *Review of child development research. Vol. 7: The family*. Chicago: University of Chicago Press.

Seligman, M. (1983). *The family with a handicapped child: Understanding and treatment*. New York: Grune & Stratton.

Sigel, I. E., & Laosa, L. M. (Eds.). (1983). *Changing families*. New York: Plenum.

Turnbull, A. P. (1986). *Families, professionals, and exceptionality: A special partnership*. Columbus, OH: Merrill.

Yogman, M. W., & Brazelton, T. B. (1986). *In support of families*. Cambridge, MA: Harvard University Press.

The Individualized Family Service Plan

The Individualized Family Service Plan (IFSP) is a new requirement of P.L. 99-457. Public Law 94-142 requires a written Individualized Education Plan (IEP) for each child eligible for special education and related services, and this requirement of an IFSP is a logical extension of that requirement.

The IFSP must be in writing and it must contain

- a statement of the infant's or toddler's present levels of functioning in the behavior domains;

- a statement of the family's strengths and needs;

- the major outcomes to be expected for the child and the family;

- the criteria, procedures, and time lines to be used in determining child and family progress;

- a description of the specific early intervention services needed to meet the child's and his or her family's needs, including a description of the method, intensity, and frequency of service delivery;

- the case manager's name; and

- a description of any Part B of EHA transition services needed.

The IFSP must be based on child and family assessments conducted by a multidisciplinary team, and the team must include at least one of the child's parents or the child's guardian. This IFSP must be re-evaluated at least once each year, and the family is to receive a progress review of the IFSP at least every 6 months.

It is the responsibility of the lead agency to determine policies that govern the development, implementation, and monitoring of the IFSP, but that does not mean that only the lead agency is involved in developing the IFSP. In fact, the states are certain to have several options for developing IFSPs. It is possible that programs that provide early intervention services would develop the IFSP for families they serve. It is also possible that the state could contract with organizations within the state that perform assessments to carry out the required family assessments and provide this information to the agency preparing the IFSP. If this procedure is followed, it is likely that someone from the assessment unit will be asked to participate with the team that is developing the IFSP. And, it is possible that a combination of these two approaches could be utilized.

Collaborative Interagency Agreements

When a state has reached the time when it will implement the full service early intervention system it has developed, the implementation of the IFSP triggers responses by all the relevant early intervention agencies identified in the IFSP. If the IFSP calls for special instruction with both a center-based and a home-based component, the agency or agencies providing these services must begin providing them. If the IFSP calls for provision of respite care and assistance to the mother in obtaining her high school GED, the agencies providing these services must begin to provide them. All of these services have a cost associated with them, costs that must be borne by the appropriate agency within the system; thus, prior to the time when the IFSP begins to call for the delivery of services, the lead agency must have developed and put in place collaborative interagency agreements.

Under P.L. 99-457, the state's lead agency is responsible for entering into formal agreements with other agencies and entities within the state. The purpose of these agreements is to (a) establish the extent to which a particular agency will participate in the state's early intervention system, (b) define the financial responsibility of each agency for paying for early intervention services, and (c) establish procedures for resolving disputes that could occur over either service delivery or costs.

Interagency collaboration and cooperation are critical to the success of the early intervention system envisioned by the authors of P.L. 99-457. Congress did not wish to establish a new bureaucracy for this purpose; instead, it wished to support cooperation among agencies within a state, and in so doing, Congress hoped to promote more efficient use of tax dollars and more efficient use of services provided by those tax dollars.

Elder (1980) has identified a number of elements of a formal interagency agreement. These include:

1. *Statement of Purpose:* This statement should describe the purpose and goals of the interagency agreement;

2. *Definition of Terms:* Because terms can differ among agencies, the interagency agreement should identify these differences and spell out the meaning of the terms so that agencies that are party to the agreement are in accord;

3. *Program Delineation:* The agreement should describe the specific program, services, or focus for which the document is written, so that all parties know what is expected of them;

4. *First Dollar Responsibility:* The agreement should specify which agency pays for which service;

5. *Roles and Responsibilities:* To reduce confusion, the agreement should specify the roles and responsibilities of participants from each agency;

6. *Designation of Responsible Positions:* The agreement should spell out who is in charge in each participating agency; more specifically, who is in charge of implementing the agreement, of monitoring it, and of negotiating any change to the agreement;

7. *Administrative Procedures:* The collaborative agreement should describe the start and end dates of the agreement, and include a mechanism for making needed revisions. The agreement should spell out the requirements to protect the privacy of persons affected by the agreement, and all other procedures that are necessary to administer the agreement; and

8. *Evaluation Design:* Procedures should be agreed upon up front that will be used to evaluate the effectiveness of the interagency agreement in providing services.

Case Management

As a requirement of the state's early intervention system, case management services must be provided. According to Austin (1983), case management is a mechanism for connecting and coordinating various segments of a service delivery system into a comprehensive package designed to meet a client's needs. Miller (1983) describes case management as the link between the individual and a fragmented system of service delivery: "Case management is recognized as one of the most essential, if not *the* essential service, in community programs. It is viewed as a means of overcoming the complexity and fragmentation of our service system" (p. 7). Miller (1984) has also described case management as the orchestration of services, programs, and resources needed by an individual, with this mix of services, programs, and resources subject to change as the needs of the individual change.

The development of case management services can be traced to growth of human service program options in this country. As programs were created to provide more and different services to a variety of consumers in this country, their growth was essentially categorical. That is, the federal social programs created during the 1960s and early 1970s were programs that were established for a specific purpose; their structure and funding were written into the laws establishing them, and states had few options in how they implemented these programs (as opposed to a block grant program, which theoretically allows a state to decide the best mix of its block grant dollars). Also, these social programs were created without much consideration being given to the variety of other programs that were also being established by Congress and implemented by a variety of state agencies.

As a consequence, human service programs evolved into a fragmented, complex, uncoordinated, and duplicative array, and this array of services was becoming increasingly difficult to access (Intagliata, 1982). Consequently, the Department of Health, Education, and Welfare in the 1970s funded a series of projects that were designed to find means to better coordinate and allow access to this array of human service programs. Called "service integration projects," these projects focused on such activities as client tracking, information and referral systems, interagency planning, and other strategies that might be useful in combating the problems caused by the growth and fragmentation of these human service programs. Case management was a strategy that emerged from this series of projects.

Case management also received attention as a result of the movement to deinstitutionalize persons. As those formerly institutionalized were released into communities, it soon became obvious that these persons did not have the skills needed to deal with multiple bureaucracies. Case management services were recommended to resolve this problem: Case management was seen as helpful in ensuring (a) continuity in care across services; (b) that services would be responsive to the variety of a person's needs and to changes in those needs over time; (c) access to the needed services; and (d) that the services provided would match the needs of the person receiving them (Intagliata, 1982).

According to the 1987 *Encyclopedia of Social Work* (Minahan, 1987), there are four basic functions to case management. These are:

1. *assessment,* to provide information about client needs and their potential strengths and weaknesses. Case managers are not necessarily expected to conduct routine assessments but they are expected to be knowledgeable about assessments of their clients.

2. *planning,* to ensure that each client has an overall case plan that lists services to be received, when and how they are to be delivered, and how the services are to be linked together in a comprehensive manner.

3. *linking,* so that clients receive the services that are necessary to meet their needs, and this function can include advocacy by the case manager for their clients.

4. *monitoring,* not only of how well the services are being delivered but also of how well the client is working within the service delivery system.

More recently, Garland, Woodruff, and Buck (1988) have identified six common case management tasks: (a) assessing client needs, (b) developing service plans, (c) coordinating service delivery, (d) monitoring service delivery, (e) evaluating services, and (f) advocating on behalf of the needs and rights of the client.

In the state's early intervention system, the person named to be case manager is intended to be the person who is best qualified to fulfill that role, based on the child's needs and the needs of the family. In some cases this could be the team nurse or the physical therapist; in other cases this could be the special educator or the pediatrician or the social worker. It is also possible that the case manager could be a parent or guardian, since this is not prohibited by the law. However, should this option be exercised, it is likely that some parents would experience difficulty dealing with the various bureaucracies and with an unfamiliar array of early intervention service options. In fact, because one important function of the case manager is to link the client (in this case the family) with the needed services, one can almost assume that parents were not originally visualized as playing the role of case manager.

Regardless of who is named case manager, parents do remain in control of their child's early intervention program. Parents must agree to the package of services that is developed. If they do not like this mix, they are free to follow the state's due process procedures to change it. This is true for their concern about their child, and it is true for any concerns they might have about services that are being provided to meet parent needs.

It would be in violation of the spirit behind P.L. 99-457 if a state were to develop an early intervention case management system that did not promote empowerment of parents [see Dunst & Trivette (in press) for a comprehensive discussion of this issue]. The authors of P.L. 99-457 recognized that parents are central to any early intervention efforts, and the law reflects this recognition. The law does not envision development of a system that would have case managers "doing" for parents! Instead, the intent was to use the early intervention system to help parents take charge of the issues that affect them and their child, thus ensuring that parental empowerment should also be seen as a primary function of case management services.

Qualified Personnel

Public Law 99-457 addresses two aspects of personnel preparation with respect to the delivery of early intervention services. First, the law requires that, as part of the state's early intervention system, there must be in place a comprehensive system of personnel development. This requirement reflects awareness by Congress that early intervention personnel are likely to be in short supply initially, and therefore, each state is expected to develop a training program that includes both preservice and inservice elements. Congress intended this training to be broadly conceived and focused on all the personnel who would be involved in early intervention, including public and private service providers, individuals involved in making referrals to the early intervention system, health system personnel, special education or special instruction personnel, and others working within the state's early intervention system.

Only a few states offered early intervention services to infants and toddlers before passage of P.L. 99-457. Thus, there is not likely to be a large pool of available trained personnel. In addition, few programs exist for training infant intervention personnel, and few states have credentialing requirements for infant and toddler intervention personnel. Thus, prior to P.L. 99-457, the incentives for developing training programs or acquiring training in this area were lacking. To provide the reader with information about existing programs or models for training qualified infant intervention personnel, several resources are listed below. The reader also will likely find these resources useful to any discussions dealing with credentialing of infant interventionists.

Preparing Qualified Personnel

Bailey, D. B., Farel, A. M., O'Donnell, K. J., Simeonsson, R. J., & Miller, C. A. (1986). Preparing infant interventionists: Inderdepartmental training in special education and maternal and child health. *Journal of the Division of Early Childhood, 11*(1), 67–77.

Burke, P. J., McLaughlin, M. J., & Valdivieson, C. H. (1988). Preparing professionals to educate handicapped infants and young children: Some policy considerations. *Topics in Early Childhood Special Education, 8*(1), 73–80.

Geik, I., Gilkerson, L., & Sponseller, D. B. (1982). An early intervention training model. *Journal of the Division for Early Childhood, 5*, 42–52.

Harbin, G. (1988). Implementation of P.L. 99-457: State technical assistance needs. *Topics in Early Childhood Special Education, 8*(1), 24–36.

Hobbs, N., & Perrin, J. (1985). *Issues in the care of children with chronic illness.* San Francisco: Jossey-Bass.

Mallory, B. (1983). The preparation of early childhood special educators: A model program. *Journal of the Division for Early Childhood, 7,* 32–40.

McCollum, J. A. W. (1982). Teaching teachers to teach: A framework for pre-service program planning. *Journal of the Division for Early Childhood, 6,* 52–59.

McLaughlin, M. J., Smith-Davis, J., & Burke, P. J. (1986). *Personnel to educate the handicapped in America: A status report.* College Park: Institute for the Study of Exceptional Children and Youth, The University of Maryland.

Smith, B. J., & Powers, C. (1987). Issues related to developing state certification policies. *Topics in Early Childhood Special Education, 7*(3), 12–23.

Stile, S. W., Abernathy, S. M., Pettibone, T. J., & Wachtel, W. J. (1984). Training and certification for early childhood special education personnel: A six-year follow-up study. *Journal of the Division for Early Childhood, 8,* 69–73.

The second personnel issue discussed in the law addresses the issue of the qualifications of early intervention personnel. Because delivery of early intervention services can occur across a variety of settings and agencies, Congress wanted to ensure that personnel who were early interventionists employed by one agency were as qualified as similar personnel working in a different agency. For example, a special educator must meet state certification requirements to deliver special instruction to children. An employee of a state mental retardation agency might deliver similar services but not be required to possess similar credentials. Therefore, the law requires a state to develop and implement policies and procedures to ensure that all early intervention personnel are appropriately and adequately trained. (The reader may wish to review the regulations material in Chapter 2 about this topic.)

In addition to the personnel training requirements specified in P.L. 99-457, the law includes a requirement that the state establish and maintain standards that are consistent with any state approved or recognized certification, licensing, registration, or other comparable requirements that apply to the area in which personnel are providing early intervention services. If a state's existing standards for early intervention personnel qualifications are not based on the highest requirements in the state for that profession, the state must show what steps it is taking to retrain personnel or to hire personnel that meet appropriate professional requirements in the state.

4

Components of a Comprehensive
Data Collection System

Public Law 99-457 identifies 14 minimum components that should be a part of a state's comprehensive early intervention system. Most of these components pertain to services that must be delivered to children, or to assurances that a state must provide to the federal government. The final component required by this law is a data collection system that would compile data describing the functioning of the comprehensive system. Such a data collection system must have as its foundation the collection of reliable, valid data from early intervention programs and related agencies throughout a state.

While states have been providing data to the federal government on services to school-aged handicapped children for many years, the variety of agencies contributing to those reports has been relatively limited. Typically such agencies include private school districts, local and regional special education agencies, schools for the handicapped, and so forth. Most of these agencies already provide data to the state for other purposes. The passage of P.L. 99-457 in 1986 dramatically increased the complexity of data reporting tasks because it mandates design (and reporting) of a comprehensive interagency *system* in settings in which no such system had previously existed.

The designated lead agency in each state must gather reliable, valid, common data from agencies that may have little or no prior experience with common reporting requirements that cut across a variety of agencies and programs. Interagency agreements must be established to permit collection of such common data from agencies with little or no formal reporting responsibilities to the lead agency. For example, a state's Department of Mental Health may be a designated lead agency. This agency has an established data collection system designed for its own purposes. Under the state's Early Intervention System, the lead agency must also obtain data from programs such as those operated by the Society for Crippled Children; the state Maternal and Child Health Office; and the state Department of Health. It is likely that each of these other agencies also already has established data collection procedures that will vary from those of the lead agency. This chapter has been written to assist those state and local agencies to develop the required common data system.

This chapter presents and discusses data collection tools suitable for a statewide or local comprehensive early intervention system. At least eight of the 14 components mandated by P.L. 99-457 will necessitate development of data collection tools. This text includes examples of such tools. The instruments presented in this text should be viewed as guidelines, designed to provide readers with ideas that can be used in the development of state or locally specific reporting. The instruments are as follow:

Figure 4.1: Early Intervention Services Eligibility Record
Figure 4.2: Checklist for Early Intervention Timetables
Figure 4.3: Analysis of Individualized Family Service Plans Form
Figure 4.4: Individualized Family Service Plan Form
Figure 4.5: Early Intervention Program Description
Figure 4.6: Identifying Early Intervention Resources
Figure 4.7: Early Intervention Personnel Development Form
Figure 4.8: Early Intervention Staff Characteristics Form
Figure 4.9: Early Intervention Services Report

At a minimum, the instruments in this text should, when considered together, adequately describe all federally mandated components of an early intervention system. The data generated by these instruments can provide all information required of state lead agencies per the request for information released on February 10, 1988, by the director of the Office of Special Education Programs, United States Department of Education (see Appendix 2 of this text, OSEP Memorandum, 1988). Additionally, the instruments are useful for describing state or locally funded components of such a system.

Instruments described in this text may be used as a total data collection system. Alternatively, they may be used individually or in any subsets that are of interest to state or local early intervention specialists. The instruments are designed to be used in a computerized Management Information System (MIS), although they also lend themselves to manual collation and analysis of data.

As researchers and early intervention specialists, we are familiar with the caution and reserve that typically greet data collection in early intervention settings. Many practitioners are reluctant to commit energy to the collection of data that are of primary use for administrative reporting. Our experience indicates, however, that high-quality data collection is possible when requests for data are timely, consistent in language and tone, and clear in directions and intent. We have built these concerns into the instruments described in this text.

We also encourage early intervention administrators to share the reports generated by data collection systems with the practitioners providing data to those systems. Such sharing serves two purposes: (a) It provides an opportunity for practitioners to identify inaccuracies in obtained data, and (b) such sharing also provides an opportunity for practitioners to see and appreciate the results of their contributions.

Component 1: A Definition of the Term Developmentally Delayed

The Required Component

Public Law 99-457 includes as its first mandated component a requirement that a statewide comprehensive system must include a definition of the term *developmentally delayed*. This definition may vary *across* states, but its definition must be consistent within each state.

Background

The comprehensive early intervention system supported by P.L. 99-457 is designed to meet the needs of three distinct groups of infants and toddlers. As of February 1988, federal reporting requirements do not mandate reporting of infants and toddlers being served under P.L. 99-457 by eligibility group (OSEP Memorandum, 1988). We anticipate, however, that subsequent reporting requirements, and states' accountability for auditing purposes, will dictate the need to monitor eligibility of infants and toddlers with a high degree of specificity. The following discussion, therefore, and subsequent instrumentation emphasize eligibility of infants and toddlers for early intervention services by each of the three distinct groups of children.

The first group of children addressed by the law includes those children from birth through age 2, inclusive, who have a diagnosed physical or mental condition that has a high probability of resulting in developmental delay. Specific determination of physical or mental conditions having high probability of resulting in developmental disability is left to the states.

Physical conditions that most states are likely to identify in their early intervention system include chromosomal abnormalities such as Down Syndrome, syndromes such as Fetal Alcohol Syndrome, neurological disorders such as cerebral palsy, sensory impairments such as deafness or blindness, congenital infections, and chronic illness. Many of these children will be diagnosed at birth, but others will be identified during infancy.

Mental conditions that most states are likely to include in their early intervention system include infantile autism, elective mutism, hyperactivity, or some form of psychosocial abnormality. Few of these children will be diagnosed at birth. Infants and toddlers with diagnosed mental conditions will be fewer in number than those with diagnosed physical conditions.

The presence of developmental delay is not required prior to onset of early intervention services, provided that such a condition (e.g., Down Syndrome) has been documented. Children with documented mental or physical conditions should be assessed for program planning purposes, but such developmental assessment should not be a part of determining eligibility for these children.

The second group eligible for services, as this component indicates, includes children from birth through age 2, inclusive, who are experiencing developmental delays. Delays must be documented using appropriate diagnostic instruments and may be in one or more of the following areas: cognitive development, physical development, language and speech development, psychosocial development, and self-help skills.

As mentioned in Chapter 3, states are able to choose from a variety of methods for determining developmental delay. Most infant assessment tools provide an indication of the level of current functioning, reporting that functioning as a Developmental Age (DA) score. The DA, measured in months, reflects the age of an average child exhibiting behavior similar to that demonstrated during testing. An 18-month-old toddler whose DA is 12 months is exhibiting behavior on a test similar to that of a typical 12-month-old. This child is actually performing at 66% of what is expected for a child of that age. States can set a cut-off score in *DA Percentages*, such as declaring that a child is developmentally delayed if his or her measured performance is 75% or less than is expected in one (or more) areas of development. A *Raw Percentage* approach can also be used with measures that do not yield DA scores, assuming that those instruments do provide some quantitative estimate of expected performance for a typical child (e.g., the average child may be expected to score 100 on an instrument).

A few infant assessment tools (e.g., the *Bayley Scales of Infant Development*, Bayley, 1969) also yield a Standard Score for a child being tested and an expected Standard Score for a typical child of any given age. The Bayley Scales yield a mental performance Standard Score of 100 for a typical child. Instruments that provide standard scores usually also provide an estimate of the standard deviation for a test, and this standard deviation can be used with a child's Standard Score to identify a third method for categorizing developmental delay (referred to here as the *Standard Deviation* approach).

The Standard Deviation method involves comparing the standard deviation of a test to the difference obtained between the measured Standard Score for an infant and the expected Standard Score for that infant. As example, an infant whose Standard Score on the Bayley Scales is 68 would be demonstrating performance 2 standard deviations below the mean of 100 on the Bayley Scales, because the standard deviation for that test is 16 (100 expected − 68 actual = 32 points). Two standard deviations (for the Bayley Scales) is 32 (2 × 16).

The state of Indiana's Early Intervention Plan declares a child to be developmentally delayed if a measured delay is 1.5 standard deviations below expectation in at least one area of development or 1 standard deviation below expectation in two or more areas of development. Other states have adopted similar approaches to the use of a Standard Score.

Almost all instruments that provide a Standard Score also provide a Developmental Age Score. In such instances, early intervention staff should be able to check the psychometric quality of instruments by examining eligibility of children under any one of the three approaches. Under ideal psychometric conditions, eligibility determinations should not vary with each strategy. When instruments yield only Developmental Ages, either the DA approach or the Percentage approach may be used. In the few instances in which an instrument does not yield a DA, only a Percentage approach may be possible.

The third group of individuals addressed by P.L. 99-457 includes (at the discretion and definition of each state) children from birth through 2 years, inclusive, who are *at risk* of having substantial developmental delays if early intervention services are not provided. In general, there are two types of risk status: children at risk by virtue of biological factors, and children at risk by virtue of environmental factors.

Biological risk factors include low birth weight, prenatal or perinatal complications, infections or illness during neonatal or infancy stages, growth deficiencies, and so forth (see Table 3.3). Assessment of biological risk will rely heavily upon the diagnostic skills of health care professionals.

Environmental risk factors might include having a mentally ill or retarded parent, having a teenage mother, documentation of abuse or neglect, having a parent who abuses substances such as drugs or alcohol (see Table 3.3).

In Indiana, infants and toddlers with a mentally retarded parent are considered eligible for early intervention services under P.L. 99-457. As mentioned earlier, states may, at their discretion, provide services to infants and toddlers at risk. We expect wide differences from state to state in defining and serving these children and families. Elsewhere (Sheehan & Sites, in press) we discuss the complexity of assessing environmental risk. To date, most states have been hesitant to allow agencies to share data reflecting environmental risk factors. Under P.L. 99-457, a mental health agency treating a parent for alcoholism may now have to work closely with local early intervention personnel, provided that the state has identified infants of alcoholic parents as eligible for early intervention services. The interagency agreements discussed in Chapter 3 must clarify obligations and protections for data collection and dissemination in this area.

By definition, children who are determined to be developmentally delayed should also not be categorized as at risk even if accepted risk conditions are known to exist. For example, a developmentally delayed infant with a mentally retarded parent should be recognized for purposes of P.L. 99-457 as developmentally delayed. A normally functioning toddler with a mentally retarded parent could be served (at state discretion) under P.L. 99-457 by virtue of being at risk for substantial developmental delay.

It is conceivable that an infant might be classified at 6 months as at risk for developmental delay because of documented abuse or neglect and then reclassified for reporting purposes at 18 months of age as developmentally delayed. It is also conceivable that an infant or toddler might first be determined to be developmentally delayed, and subsequently categorized as having a diagnosed physical or mental condition. This might occur with a toddler who shows delays in language and speech development and later is determined to be profoundly deaf. When this occurs, the child should, for data collection purposes, be reclassified from developmentally delayed to having a documented physical condition.

Reporting Priorities

Public Law 99-457 and our knowledge of child development imply a distinct reporting priority for the three groups of children. This priority is as follows:

Highest reporting priority – Documented Conditions
Second highest reporting priority – Developmental Delay
Lowest reporting priority – At Risk

We hasten to point out that a reporting priority is *not* related to a service priority. All children from birth through 2 years, inclusive, who meet a state's eligibility criteria should be served. A reporting priority simply refers to the way in which an infant or toddler should be classified, or reclassified, for reporting purposes. No children should be counted more than once in reporting under P.L. 99-457.

The congressional authors of P.L. 99-457 firmly believed in the importance of continuous early intervention for eligible children. Once an infant or toddler becomes eligible for services, by virtue of a diagnosed handicapping condition, developmental delay, or risk status, Congress did not intend for a child to lose eligibility as a result of some change relative to those eligibility criteria. For example, a 9-month-old infant who is performing at 60% of developmental age should not be denied services 12 months later when that child's performance has increased to 73% of developmental age. Similarly, in states serving at-risk infants, an infant who has been abused for the first 6 months of life should not lose eligibility because that child is placed with loving foster parents or is legally adopted by nurturant, supportive parents.

Changes in reporting status under P.L. 99-457 should be made only to assist early intervention providers to correctly track the three groups of children addressed by the federal law. Public Law 99-457 is very clear in its intent that services to infants and toddlers should begin and continue while any administrative issues (such as changes in status) are being resolved.

Instrumentation

The instrument presented in Figure 4.1 is an example of the types of information that any administrative group (e.g., a state-designated lead agency) might request of intervention programs receiving P.L. 99-457 Part H funds. Recall our earlier mention that this instrument, and all instruments presented in this text, is intended to be a guideline, designed to help readers develop their own state or locally specific instrumentation.

The form presented in Figure 4.1 permits identification of specific children being served (by code number, name, and age), as well as reporting of the developmental delay, handicapping condition, or risk status of each child. The form can also be used for children who have been evaluated and determined to be in need of early intervention services but who are not yet receiving those services (see discussion below of federal reporting requirements, OSEP Memorandum, 1988).

In addition to reporting the areas of developmental delay, the instrument in Figure 4.1 requires that early intervention personnel specify the instruments used to assess such delay and the degree of delay in Developmental Age (DA) Percentages, Standard Deviations, or Raw Percentages. As mentioned previously, most states are likely to set cut-off scores for developmental delay in one of these three fashions (or permit a combination of methods).

The instrument included as Figure 4.1 also contains a section for reporting eligibility of infants and toddlers designated at risk. States and agencies may have to modify this form based upon the types of at-risk infants and toddlers being served in a state or a local area.

The form presented in Figure 4.1 can be used for initial reporting on all children, and then can be used to provide an update for new children or for children whose status has changed. Recall the earlier discussion that P.L. 99-457 implies a reporting priority from demonstrated handicapping conditions to developmental delay to at risk. In light of such a priority, any reporting system must easily accept changes in children's status.

On February 10, 1988, the United States Office of Special Education Programs announced the first required reporting (OSEP Memorandum, 1988) related to Part H of the Education of the Handicapped Act (P.L. 99-457).

Figure 4.1
EARLY INTERVENTION SERVICES ELIGIBILITY RECORD

Instructions. The purpose of this eligibility record is to provide a concise record of the eligibility of children being served in infant/toddler early intervention programs throughout the state. Children's names may, at the discretion of the program staff, be included in this recording system. In the event that a child's name is included in the recording system, program staff *must* still assign a unique identifier number to each child being served by the program. If a program chooses to only record identification numbers in this recording system, the program staff assume responsibility for maintaining a master record of children's identities and their respective identification numbers.

Most infants and toddlers eligible for service by early intervention programs will fit one of the following categories:

Reporting Priority

1	Children with a Diagnosed Physical Condition
1	Children with a Diagnosed Mental Condition
2	Children with a Measurable Developmental Delay
3	Children At Risk for Biological Factors
3	Children At Risk for Environmental Factors

Each infant or toddler eligible in one of the above categories should be recorded on the following recording system. In the event that a child is eligible for services in more than one category, record that child in the highest reporting priority category appropriate for that child (1, Highest Priority = Diagnosed Condition; 2, Second Highest Priority = Developmentally Delayed; 3, Lowest Priority = At Risk). A subsequent instrument, the Early Intervention Services Report, will be used to indicate whether children are actually receiving intervention services and the nature and extent of those services.

Program Title: _____ ID: _____

Program Address: _____

Person Completing This Record: _____

Telephone During Day: (_____) _____
              Area   Number

Date of Submission (or Update): _____ / _____ / _____

Figure 4.1 (Continued)

Verifying Eligibility of Children with a DIAGNOSED PHYSICAL CONDITION

NAME	ID	PROGRAM ENTRANCE DATE	BIRTH DATE	SYNDROME/ CONDITION	NEUROLOGICAL DISORDER	SENSORY IMPAIRMENT	CONGENITAL INFECTION
		__/__/__	__/__/__				
		__/__/__	__/__/__				
		__/__/__	__/__/__				
		__/__/__	__/__/__				
		__/__/__	__/__/__				

EXPLAIN EXACT CONDITION BELOW IN APPROPRIATE COLUMN

OTHER (specify) _____

OTHER (specify) _____

OTHER (specify) _____

OTHER (specify) _____

OTHER (specify) _____

CONTINUE THIS PAGE AS NECESSARY

Figure 4.1 (Continued)
Verifying Eligibility of Children with a DIAGNOSED MENTAL CONDITION

NAME	ID	PROGRAM ENTRANCE DATE	BIRTH DATE	EXPLAIN EXACT CONDITION BELOW
		__/__/__	__/__/__	
		__/__/__	__/__/__	
		__/__/__	__/__/__	
		__/__/__	__/__/__	
		__/__/__	__/__/__	
		__/__/__	__/__/__	
		__/__/__	__/__/__	
		__/__/__	__/__/__	
		__/__/__	__/__/__	

Note: In time, a state or local agency may be able to develop a diagnostic coding scheme for infants' and toddlers' mental conditions. Due to the relative recency of early intervention efforts with these children, we prefer at this time to request explanation of each condition.

CONTINUE THIS PAGE AS NECESSARY

Figure 4.1 (Continued)
Verifying Eligibility of Children with a MEASURABLE DELAY

NAME	ID	PROGRAM ENTRANCE DATE	BIRTH DATE	TOOLS MEASURING DELAY INSTRUMENT/ SUBTEST(s)	AREA OF DELAY*	NUMBER STANDARD DEVIATION DELAY	PERCENT DA DELAY	PERCENT RAW DELAY
___	__	__/__/__	__/__/__	_____	____	____ s.d.	___ %	___ %
				_____	____	____ s.d.	___ %	___ %
				_____	____	____ s.d.	___ %	___ %
				_____	____	____ s.d.	___ %	___ %
				_____	____	____ s.d.	___ %	___ %
				_____	____	____ s.d.	___ %	___ %
				_____	____	____ s.d.	___ %	___ %
___	__	__/__/__	__/__/__	_____	____	____ s.d.	___ %	___ %
				_____	____	____ s.d.	___ %	___ %
				_____	____	____ s.d.	___ %	___ %
				_____	____	____ s.d.	___ %	___ %
				_____	____	____ s.d.	___ %	___ %

*Specify each area of delay using the following code and indicate degree of delay for each area. Areas of Delay: 1 = Cognitive; 2 = Fine Motor; 3 = Gross Motor; 4 = Receptive Communication; 5 = Expressive Communication; 6 = Social/Emotional; 7 = Self-Help.

CONTINUE THIS PAGE AS NECESSARY

Figure 4.1 (Continued)
Verifying Eligibility of Children Designated BIOLOGICALLY AT RISK

NAME	ID	PROGRAM ENTRANCE DATE	BIRTH DATE	LOW BIRTH WEIGHT (grams)	PRENATAL/ PERINATAL/ NEONATAL FACTOR	INFECTION/ ILLNESS	GROWTH DEFICIENCY/ NUTRITION
		_/_/_	_/_/_				
		_/_/_	_/_/_				
		_/_/_	_/_/_				
		_/_/_	_/_/_				
		_/_/_	_/_/_				

EXPLAIN EXACT RISK FACTOR BELOW IN APPROPRIATE COLUMN

OTHER (specify) _____

OTHER (specify) _____

OTHER (specify) _____

OTHER (specify) _____

OTHER (specify) _____

CONTINUE THIS PAGE AS NECESSARY

Figure 4.1 (Continued)

Verifying Eligibility of Children Designated ENVIRONMENTALLY AT RISK

CHECK RISK FACTOR BELOW IN APPROPRIATE COLUMN

NAME	ID	PROGRAM ENTRANCE DATE	BIRTH DATE	MENTALLY RETARDED PARENT	MENTALLY ILL PARENT	ADOLESCENT PARENT	ABUSE/ NEGLECT
___	___	_/_/_	_/_/_	OTHER (specify) ___	___	___	___
___	___	_/_/_	_/_/_	OTHER (specify) ___	___	___	___
___	___	_/_/_	_/_/_	OTHER (specify) ___	___	___	___
___	___	_/_/_	_/_/_	OTHER (specify) ___	___	___	___
___	___	_/_/_	_/_/_	OTHER (specify) ___	___	___	___
___	___	_/_/_	_/_/_	OTHER (specify) ___	___	___	___

CONTINUE THIS PAGE AS NECESSARY

This memorandum, including five reporting tables, is presented in Appendix 2 of this text. Table 1 of this form, to be completed by lead agencies, requires that lead agencies report the number of infants and toddlers *receiving* early intervention services by December 1 of each year, by the following age groupings:

birth–12 months
12 months–24 months
24 months–36 months

Federal reporting also requires a single estimate (one not broken out by age) of infants and toddlers *in need of* early intervention services. These are children who have been evaluated and determined to be in need of early intervention services who were not receiving these services on December 31 of the reporting year. As mentioned earlier, current reporting requirements do not mandate identification of children by eligibility category; however, state-designated lead agencies or any local agencies will, for accountability purposes, want to obtain primary data on children's eligibility. The Eligibility Record described in Figure 4.1 provides a means for gathering such data. The Eligibility Record (discussed below) is to be used if a child is *eligible* for services. A subsequent form, the Early Intervention Services Report (see Component 14 in this chapter), is used to record actual intervention services provided to children.

Linkages with Other Instruments

The instrument presented in Figure 4.1, the Early Intervention Services Eligibility Record, includes several instances of unique identifier information that will help link eligibility data for specific children with any other data subsequently gathered for those children (e.g., number of hours of speech therapy received by a child). Such linking is possible, provided that a consistent identifier number is recorded for children in each early intervention program and that identifier codes for early intervention programs are consistently applied by the state, or by program staff.

In addition to provision for a child identification number, the Eligibility Record also permits recording a child's name and birth date. The option for provision of such information is built into many of the instruments included in this text as a check for accuracy and as insurance in the likelihood that an identifier number is incorrectly assigned or missing. Appropriate linkages with other instruments can be made when there is a match among a child's identification code, name, and birth date. When a match occurs on only one or two of those variables, an effort should be made to determine and correct the possible source of such an incomplete match (e.g., a child's last name may have been changed, or a clerical error in entering a birth date may have been made).

Suggested Methods for Data Coding and Analysis

The Early Intervention Services Eligibility Record can be manually coded or it can be computerized with either a data-based management program (such as DBase III+® or Symphony®) or a spread-sheet program (e.g., Lotus 123® or Excell®). Our experience with this form is in using it in computerized form with DBase III+. We prefer to enter data through "Screens," which are customized screen images designed to look as much like the original data reporting form as possible. We have designed computer programs to automatically check an identifier number with existing data from the same intervention program. Readers with only minimal computer background can write such a "Locate and Display" program. Such checking points out if an error has been made in assigning two children the same code number. Alternatively, such checking reveals if data being coded represent an update on an individual child (e.g., change of status from at risk to developmentally delayed). We also automatically check for congruence of birth date and name for children on whom changes of status are being made.

Specific data analyses are most often determined by the concerns of particular agencies. For federal reporting purposes, numbers of children receiving early intervention services and those eligible but not yet receiving such services must be reported to the Office of Special Education Programs (OSEP Memorandum, 1988) by December 1 of each reporting year. Analyses should be performed to yield the number of children served by year of age (as of December 1). There are no current requirements for federal reporting by type of eligibility category nor must eligible, but unserved, children be reported by age.

Component 2: Timetables for Ensuring that Services Are Available

The Required Component

To ensure rapid and consistent establishment of comprehensive early intervention systems, P.L. 99-457 requires that each state plan include timetables for ensuring that appropriate early intervention services will be available to all handicapped infants and toddlers before the beginning of the fifth year of a state's participation in the program. Further, P.L. 99-457 specifies that the comprehensive statewide Early Intervention System must be in place by the beginning of the fourth year; however, during the fourth year, the statewide system is required only to conduct multidisciplinary assessments, develop individualized family service plans, and make available case management services.

Instrumentation

Figure 4.2, a Checklist for Early Intervention Timetables, has been developed to assist state-designated lead agencies in establishing appropriate timetables. This checklist captures the major aspects of mandated P.L. 99-457 activity, although readers will likely expand the checklist to accommodate needs in their individual states.

Component 3: Timely, Comprehensive, Multidisciplinary Evaluations

The Required Component

Public Law 99-457 requires that a state's Early Intervention System include timely, comprehensive, multidisciplinary evaluation of the functioning of each handicapped infant and toddler. Also required is an assessment of the needs of families to assist in the development of their handicapped infant or toddler. This comprehensive evaluation of children's status and families' needs is to occur once per year with a 6-month review and should be a part of the mandated Individualized Family Service Plan (see Component 4, next section).

Background

The first part of this component, comprehensive evaluation of infants' and toddlers' functioning, is very similar to the requirement of appropriate assessment for handicapped school-aged children found in P.L. 94-142. The authors of P.L. 99-457 clearly valued the information gained from multidisciplinary assessment and believe that such assessment should be a bridge to early intervention (Wachs & Sheehan, 1988b).

Areas of functioning that must be included in this assessment are physical development, cognitive development, language and speech development, psycho-

Figure 4.2
CHECKLIST FOR EARLY INTERVENTION TIMETABLES

Instructions. The purpose of this checklist is to ensure that states establish realistic and appropriate timetables for establishing and implementing a statewide comprehensive early intervention system. This instrument should be circulated in draft version to appropriate state and local agencies. Items should be added to (but not deleted from) the draft. Once a final checklist is established, the checklist should be recirculated to state and local agencies for purposes of establishing realistic timelines.

State: _____

State-Designated Lead Agency: _____   Person Completing This Checklist: _____

Date Checklist Completed or Updated: _____   Telephone During Day: (_____) _____
                                                                                  Area   Number

ACTIVITY	YEAR				
	1	2	3	4	5
Define *diagnosed physical and mental conditions*	___	___	___	___	___
Define *developmental delay*	___	___	___	___	___
Define *at risk*	___	___	___	___	___
Determine whether or not to serve *at risk*	___	___	___	___	___
Develop due process procedures	___	___	___	___	___
Develop local contractor agreements	___	___	___	___	___
Implement local contractor agreements	___	___	___	___	___
Assess state needs	___	___	___	___	___

Figure 4.2 (Continued)

ACTIVITY	1	2	YEAR 3	4	5
Develop standards for personnel involved in early intervention programs	—	—	—	—	—
Train personnel	—	—	—	—	—
Enact state policy	—	—	—	—	—
Identify sources of fiscal support	—	—	—	—	—
Identify early intervention resources in the state	—	—	—	—	—
Identify gaps in early intervention service provision	—	—	—	—	—
Develop plans to close gaps in early intervention service provisions	—	—	—	—	—
Develop interagency collaborative agreements	—	—	—	—	—
Develop procedures for determining agency fiscal responsibility	—	—	—	—	—
Develop interagency and intra-agency dispute resolution procedure	—	—	—	—	—
If appropriate, consult with representative Native American Indians	—	—	—	—	—
Develop procedures for timely reimbursement of funds from one agency to another	—	—	—	—	—
Develop public awareness program	—	—	—	—	—
Implement public awareness program	—	—	—	—	—

Figure 4.2 (Continued)

ACTIVITY	YEAR				
	1	2	3	4	5
Develop comprehensive child-find system, with appropriate referral time lines	—	—	—	—	—
Establish a central directory	—	—	—	—	—
Develop case management procedures	—	—	—	—	—
Implement case management procedures	—	—	—	—	—
Develop procedures governing development of Individualized Family Service Plans	—	—	—	—	—
Implement procedures governing development of Individualized Family Service Plans	—	—	—	—	—
Develop comprehensive data system	—	—	—	—	—
Implement comprehensive data system	—	—	—	—	—

social development, and self-help skills. Assessment of these domains must be based on acceptable objective criteria. Disciplines likely to contribute to such an assessment include pediatricians, developmental psychologists, educational specialists, speech and language personnel, physical and occupational therapists, nurses, and social workers.

Numerous authors have spoken to the strengths (Gradel, 1988; Robinson & Fieber, 1988) and weaknesses (Garwood, 1981; Sheehan & Sites, in press) of existing infant measures for purposes of program planning. Few standardized instruments were developed for purposes of planning intervention programs for infants and toddlers. Such a purpose dictates that an instrument have many items, each of which is of relevance to intervention activity. Such an instrument should also be useful in a variety of settings (e.g., home, pediatric clinic) and be able to be administered by diverse intervention agents (e.g., parents, child life specialists, teachers). Few single instruments meet all these criteria; therefore, there is a need for a battery of measures to ensure that this component is an integral part of a comprehensive early intervention system. Readers are referred to recent publications (Bricker, 1982; Fewell, 1983; Guralnick & Bennett, 1987; Hanson, 1984; Wachs & Sheehan, 1988a) for guidance in selecting instruments for such a battery.

The second part of this component, assessment of family needs as they relate to enhancing children's development, is a new perspective that has been added to mandatory assessment by P.L. 99-457. Elsewhere (Sheehan & Sites, in press) we discuss the fact that assessment of family needs for enhancement of children's development is an undeveloped area. For measuring parents' knowledge of their child's development, professionals may be able to borrow measures from college and high school courses on child development and exceptional education. Several assessment tools (e.g., *Developmental Profile*, Alpern & Shearer, 1980) are designed to permit parents to report their knowledge of their infant or toddler (see also Bricker, Squires, Kaminski, & Monents, in press).

We are less optimistic about ready availability of instruments to assess the needs of parents and family members. As discussed in Chapter 3, assessment of family needs ranges from assessment of family members' knowledge of child development to assessment of needs for marital help, GED completion or job training, psychotherapy, and so forth.

Dunst (personal communication, 1988) approaches family needs assessment by assessing the strength and complexity of families' network of resources. Such assessment determines who parents might call for respite care or for advice on a child's needs. Such assessment also examines communication patterns of family members, under the assumption that families with strong communication will be better able to meet the needs of their children than families with disjointed patterns of communication. Readers are also referred to the work of Winton and Turnbull (1981) and Bristol (1987) for assistance in building such approaches into their comprehensive early intervention systems.

Sheehan and Sites (in press) have recently spoken to issues in assessing needs of families in which at-risk children are receiving early intervention services. Family assessment may be actively resisted if children have been abused or neglected, and there are few guidelines about the protection of such data. For example, can a noncustodial parent claim access to needs assessment data indicating that a custodial parent has a multitude of parenting needs? Are data on a parent's alcoholism treatment to be included in an IFSP? Progress in such treatment surely relates to the ability of that parent to facilitate his or her child's development. These and related questions must be faced in the near future by states and intervention specialists across the nation.

Instrumentation

The federally mandated component of P.L. 99-457 pertaining to timely evaluations of children's developmental status and family needs places this activity in the development and review of the Individualized Family Service Plan (IFSP). The instrument presented in Figure 4.3 is a form developed to conduct a thorough review of such IFSPs on a periodic basis. Persons using this form can review every child's IFSP in an intervention program, or they can review a sampling of IFSPs. Similarly, state and local agencies could mandate that the form presented in Figure 4.3 be completed by intervention specialists and placed on file with the IFSP for every child. As Figure 4.3 indicates, children are identified by code number, birth date, and name if desired.

For federal reporting purposes, state-designated lead agencies must report the number of children from birth through 2 years who receive psychological services (such as comprehensive evaluations or re-evaluations) under P.L. 99-457 (OSEP Memorandum, 1988; see Appendix 2). These data can be obtained by applying the Analysis of Individualized Family Service Plans to all existing IFSPs within a state. These data will also be yielded by the Early Intervention Services Report, discussed under Component 14 in this chapter.

Linkages with Other Instruments

The Analysis of Individualized Family Service Plans can be directly linked to the Early Intervention Services Eligibility Record as the same coding system for programs and children would be employed. (The Early Intervention Services Report, discussed under Component 14 in this chapter, also uses the same coding system for programs and children.)

Figure 4.3
ANALYSIS OF INDIVIDUALIZED FAMILY SERVICE PLANS

Instructions. The purpose of this instrument is to review the content of *each* infant's or toddler's Individualized Family Service Plan. Children's names may, at the discretion of the early intervention program staff, be included in this analysis. In the event that a child's name is included in the analysis, program staff *must* still assign a unique identifier number to each child being served by the demonstration program. If any early intervention program chooses to only record identification numbers in the analysis, the program staff assume responsibility for maintaining a master record of children's identities and their respective identification numbers.

Program Title: _____

Program Address: _____

Person Completing This Analysis: _____

Telephone During Day: (_____) _____
              Area   Number

Date of Analysis: _____ / _____ / _____

Child's Name: _____ Child's ID: _____ Birth Date: ____ / ____ / ____

Child has an IFSP _____ Yes _____ No   If yes, go on.

IFSP Component	Yes	No
1. Child's name is on the form.	____	____
2. Parents' names are on the form.	____	____
3. Contains report of multidisciplinary assessment of child.	____	____
4. Parents participated in the IFSP development (documented on the IFSP).	____	____

Figure 4.3 (Continued)

IFSP Component	Yes	No
5. IFSP reviewed with the parents in the past 6 months.	___	___
6. Multidisciplinary assessment occurred in a reasonable time after the initial referral (e.g., 4 weeks).	___	___
7. Contains present level of infant's:		
a. physical development	___	___
b. cognitive development	___	___
c. language/communication development	___	___
d. psychosocial development	___	___
e. self-help skill acquisition	___	___
8. Statement of families' strengths and needs is contained in the IFSP.	___	___
9. Statement of major outcomes to be achieved by the parents, with criteria and time lines, is contained in the IFSP.	___	___
10. Statement of the nature and intensity of the service provided to infants and parents is contained in the IFSP.	___	___
11. Projected or actual dates of initiation of services are contained.	___	___
12. Case manager is named.	___	___
Please state that person's title: _____		
13. Statement for supporting transition to other agencies if needed is contained.	___	___

Suggested Methods for Data Coding and Analysis

The data gathered by the Analysis of Individualized Family Service Plans represent minimum mandated components of an IFSP. Data obtained from this review can be used for federal reporting of the number of children receiving psychological services. Such data can also be used to identify intervention programs that fail to conduct comprehensive, multidisciplinary assessments. These data could also be used to identify service gaps or problems with time lines and to direct inservice training efforts on programatic assessment as well as assessment of family needs.

Component 4: Development of Individualized Family Service Plans

The Required Component

Public Law 99-457 states as a fourth minimum component of a comprehensive early intervention system that the system must contain for each infant and toddler an Individualized Family Service Plan (IFSP) including case management services. Further, this IFSP must be evaluated yearly and reviewed with families every 6 months.

Background

The origins of P.L. 99-457's concern for an IFSP are certainly to be found in the Individualized Education Plan required by P.L. 94-142 for school-aged and preschool children. IFSPs must be developed with parents and must be preserved in written form, two requirements identical to those of IEPs. Periodic reviews and evaluations of the IFSP must occur, in a fashion similar to that of IEPs. To avoid any delays in initiation of intervention, services can, with the permission of parents, begin before the IFSP is completed. This reflects the P.L. 99-457 authors' belief that infant development is relatively rapid, thus administrative concerns should not delay the onset of early intervention.

As mentioned earlier, IFSPs must contain an evaluation of an infant's or toddler's present levels of developmental functioning, and an assessment of family needs as they relate to enhancing children's development. In fashion similar to the long- and short-term objectives of P.L. 94-142, the new law, P.L. 99-457, requires that major expected outcomes for the child and family must be stated in writing. Additionally, criteria, procedures, and time lines used to determine progress toward achieving those objectives must be made clear. The IFSP must also contain a clear statement of early intervention services to be received by each child and his or her family, including the frequency, intensity, method, and time line of delivering these services.

The case management responsibilities must be made clear in the IFSP, and the law states that the case manager must be from the profession most closely associated with an infant's or toddler's developmental needs. Finally, the steps to be taken to support transition of infants and toddlers to preschool intervention services, if they are likely to be necessary, must be made clear in each child's IFSP.

Similarities between IEPs and IFSPs are very obvious. We point out, though, that IFSP development may be the responsibility of many professionals who have not had experience with IEPs. This will occur because the comprehensive early intervention systems being created under P.L. 99-457 will be broader in scope, involving a more diverse group of professionals. We also point out that the addition of a family needs assessment component represents a challenging new activity for educators who have focused on the child as their sole target for assessment.

There are no formal reporting requirements established (yet) for IFSPs. As mentioned in the previous component, one small part of an IFSP is a reporting of comprehensive evaluations performed for each child, and this activity must be reported on Table 2 of the required federal reporting (OSEP Memorandum, 1988). Existence of a complete IFSP and due process as it relates to IFSPs are, for the present, a monitoring concern of lead agencies and local agencies. Any comprehensive early intervention system, with clearly documented IFSP components, must contain some review procedures, and these are discussed below.

Instrumentation

Figure 4.4 is a model form for an Individualized Family Service Plan (IFSP). This model form meets all requirements specified for IFSPs in P.L. 99-457.

Linkages with Other Instruments

The Individualized Family Service Plan Form, presented as Figure 4.4, uses the same format and coding scheme for children and programs as do the other forms presented in this text. Children's records might be sampled from any of the child-specific forms presented in this text, and a complete recording of all available data might be requested and reviewed.

Figure 4.4
INDIVIDUALIZED FAMILY SERVICE PLAN FORM

Instructions. This form must be completed at onset of early intervention (or as soon as possible thereafter) for every infant and toddler in the program. The form is to be completed with the full participation of children's parents and staff, and parents are expected to sign and date the form when it is complete. The form is to be reviewed after 6 months (again, signatures are necessary) and revised, as needed, after 12 months.

Child's Name _____ Child's ID: _____ Birth Date: _____ / _____ / _____

Date IFSP Completed: _____ / _____ / _____

Early Intervention Program Staff Completing IFSP:

_____ _____
Signature   Discipline

_____ _____
Signature   Discipline

_____ _____
Signature   Discipline

_____ _____
Signature   Discipline

Parent(s): I (We) have reviewed the Individualized Family Service Plan and approve of this plan.

_____ _____ / _____ / _____
Signature   Date

_____ _____ / _____ / _____
Signature   Date

Figure 4.4 (Continued)

Part I: CHILD ASSESSMENT

Present Level of Functioning

Instruments/Procedures

1. Physical Development: _____

2. Cognitive Development: _____

3. Speech /Language Development: _____

4. Psychosocial Development: _____

5. Self-Help Skills: _____

Part II: FAMILY ASSESSMENT   Family Members: _____

A. Family Strengths

Method Used to Assess

1. _____

2. _____

3. _____

B. Family Needs, as Expressed by Family

1. _____

2. _____

3. _____

Figure 4.4 (Continued)

Part III: TEAM RECOMMENDATIONS FOR SERVICES TO CHILD/FAMILY

1. _____

2. _____

3. _____

Part IV: MAJOR EXPECTED CHILD OUTCOMES

1. Outcome: _____

   a. Intervention Procedures/Services: _____

   b. Assessment Criteria, Procedures: _____

   c. Time Lines: _____

2. Outcome: _____

   a. Intervention Procedures/Services: _____

   b. Assessment Criteria, Procedures: _____

   c. Time Lines: _____

3. Outcome: _____

   a. Intervention Procedures/Services: _____

   b. Assessment Criteria, Procedures: _____

   c. Time Lines: _____

Figure 4.4 (Continued)

Part V: MAJOR EXPECTED FAMILY OUTCOMES

1. Outcome: _____

    a. Intervention Procedures/Services: _____

    b. Assessment Criteria, Procedures: _____

    c. Time Lines: _____

2. Outcome: _____

    a. Intervention Procedures/Services: _____

    b. Assessment Criteria, Procedures: _____

    c. Time Lines: _____

Part VI: ROLE OF PARENTS IN DEVELOPING THE IFSP (Optional)

Please provide a short, descriptive statement of the parents' role in developing this IFSP.

_____

_____

_____

Part VII: CASE MANAGER INFORMATION

1. Name of Case Manager: _____

2. Title of Case Manager: _____

Figure 4.4 (Continued)

Part VIII: REVIEW AND ANNUAL RE-EVALUATION AND REVISION TIME LINES

1. Date of Next Review: ___/___/___

2. Date of Next Revaluation: ___/___/___

3. Date of Next Revision of IFSP: ___/___/___

Part IX: STATEMENT OF ANTICIPATED TRANSITION SERVICES

Suggested Methods for Data Coding and Analysis

The data for the IFSP form presented in Figure 4.4 may be gathered and maintained as paper records in a fashion similar to the recording of most Individualized Education Plans (IEPs) in the public schools. Figure 4.4 can also be computerized using data-based management screen entry for those early intervention programs having ready access to microcomputers.

Data analysis can be as simple as checking to ensure the existence of mandated components of IFSPs (also, see Figure 4.3 for this purpose) or as complex as an analysis of communalities of treatment programs across an entire early intervention agency.

Component 5: Child-Find Requirements

The Required Component

The comprehensive early intervention system supported in each state by P.L. 99-457 must include a comprehensive child-find system including a system of making referrals to service providers that includes time lines and provides for participation by primary referral sources.

Background

Child Find represents a type of affirmative action campaign designed to aggressively search for eligible handicapped children and to provide services to those children. Bourland and Harbin (1987) point out that Child Find is a term meant to refer to 10 elements of a comprehensive service delivery system. The 10 elements are (1) definition of tracking population, (2) screening and prescreening, (3) public awareness, (4) referrals, (5) tracking registries, (6) case management, (7) diagnostic assessment, (8) coordination of efforts, (9) financial resources, and (10) trained personnel.

We note that many of the elements of Child Find specified in Bourland and Harbin (1987) are to be found in other mandated components of the comprehensive early intervention system mandated by P.L. 99-457. For example, a public awareness campaign is mandated by P.L. 99-457 as Component 6. Availability of trained personnel is mandated as Component 13. Diagnostic assessment is mandated under P.L. 99-457 as Component 3.

Insight into congressional thinking with regard to Child Find is to be found in House Report 99-860 (see Chapter 2 of this text for discussion of this report). In House Report 99-860, the legislative committee introduced

Child Find by saying that a comprehensive child-find system must include a system for referrals to service providers. "The system of referrals must include timeliness and provide for the participation of primary referral sources. 'Primary referral sources' include hospitals, physicians, other health care providers, public health facilities, and day care facilities" (p. 10).

In mandating a comprehensive child-find system, congressional authors did not automatically assume that no such system was in place. In fact, Part B of the Education of the Handicapped Act (EHA) mandates such a system for preschoolers. Congressional authors of P.L. 99-457 felt that existing systems must be modified or expanded (if necessary) to be able to reach out to eligible infants and toddlers.

Instrumentation

Due to possible broad interpretation of child-find activities, and the likely existence of child-find systems for preschoolers, we do not offer a specific instrument to document the existence of a comprehensive child-find system for infants and toddlers. All instruments presented in this book, particularly the Early Intervention Services Report (Figure 4.9), do significantly relate to child-find activities.

Component 6: Public Awareness Requirements

The Required Component

The authors of P.L. 99-457 were not content to let the public develop a gradual awareness of the existence of comprehensive early intervention systems. A required component of this law is that comprehensive early intervention systems must include a public awareness program focusing on early identification of handicapped infants and toddlers.

Background

Using House Report 99-860 as a guide, the requirements of this component can be considered distinct from the child-find requirement specified in the previous component in that public awareness efforts are likely to be more general, directed at large segments of a statewide population, whereas congressional authors of P.L. 99-457 focused on a specific referral system in their discussion of Child Find (see discussion to this effect in previous component). The goal of this public awareness component of P.L. 99-457 is to ensure that anyone who encounters infants or toddlers is aware of the existence of a comprehensive early intervention system and able to contact that system for further information. Trohanis and Decker (1987) describe public awareness as representing a strategy for promoting public acceptance and raising public consciousness about the needs of handicapped infants and toddlers.

Some states are addressing this component by employing advertising/marketing firms to mount professional public awareness campaigns on television, radio, and in newspapers. Other states have employed early intervention specialists who are designing and disseminating materials such as calendars and posters displaying the developmental milestones expected of normally developing infants and toddlers. Toll-free phone numbers are provided for any person who has a question about these milestones or about a particular child's performance. Callers are then referred to local early intervention specialists for further discussion or referral.

Trohanis and Decker (1987) describe several goals of public awareness including enhanced visibility of early intervention programs, change in legislation and state policies, improved communication among (and between) agency personnel and parents, and publicization of achievements of early intervention programs.

Instrumentation

Due to the broad definition of public awareness, we do not suggest in this text a specific instrument to document the existence of those efforts. The State Technical Assistance Resource Team (START), located at the Frank Porter Graham Child Development Center at the University of North Carolina at Chapel Hill, has prepared an extensive packet of materials related to public awareness campaigns and example products of such a campaign.

Component 7: Central Directory Requirements

The Required Component

Comprehensive early intervention systems funded under P.L. 99-457 must include a central directory that contains a list of early intervention services, resources, and experts available in the state who can advise on matters of children's growth and development. Additionally, the directory should include any research and demonstration programs being conducted in the state.

Background

The requirement of a central directory represents a realistic awareness that we live in an information age, and early intervention resources must be well known to be of use to all eligible children. There are actually two thrusts to this component. The first emphasizes early intervention services, or programs. The second emphasizes experts, or people. While there will be overlap between these two thrusts, they might also be distinct. For example, an early intervention program in a particular geographic area might offer home-based services for developmentally delayed toddlers who are chronically ill. The central directory describing that program might also include an identification of the educational and medical personnel who work in the program. The central directory might also include, however, an identification of medical personnel who work individually in the same geographic area with families of handicapped infants.

The reference that has just been made to handicapped children with medical problems was intentional. One excellent example of a national central directory is the *Parent Resource Directory* published in 1988 by the Association of Children with Health Handicaps (ACHH). In light of the fragmentation of resources for children with health handicaps, this organization has been very aggressive in identifying programs and personnel who are available to work with such children.

Several guidelines in developing a central directory are worth noting. First, the target audience for the directory should be carefully considered. Is the directory to be used primarily by professionals? Are there terms that are likely to be unfamiliar to experts in other disciplines? For example, *child life specialist* is a term familiar to medical personnel but unfamiliar to teachers.

Second, a central directory must be easy to use. Alphabetical listings are likely to be of less use than geographic listings. Headings and indexes must be understandable. To ensure such ease, the format should be field-tested in a variety of settings.

Third, persons gathering information for a central directory must recognize that survey response rates go down as the amount of requested information increases. A central directory will be of little use if it represents 50% missing data. As example, a local coalition of early intervention specialists recently sent us a survey that contained several hundred items needing completion and three pages of directions. The results obtained from such a survey are likely to contain a great deal of missing information, and the obtained surveys are unlikely to represent all intervention programs in the county. Early intervention specialists and other professionals are likely to contribute information to a directory, if the request for that information is reasonably brief and simple.

Fourth, a central directory will be in need of frequent revision, probably on a yearly or biannual basis. If P.L. 99-457 is successful, early intervention programs will increase in number and change in scope. Networks of experts will be constantly forming and expertise in early intervention concerns will be growing. Such a fluid setting would suggest a need for frequent (and inexpensive) modification of a central directory.

Fifth, a mechanism must be established for disseminating the central directory to potential users. Once intervention programs and individual experts have been identified in the central directory, they will become likely targets for dissemination. A firm effort must be made, however, to see that the directory is widely disseminated, even to potential users who did not contribute to the directory.

Instrumentation

The two thrusts of a central directory, intervention programs and experts, are best addressed separately. Figure 4.5 represents an effort to gather a modest amount of information from early intervention programs throughout a state. The instrument shown in Figure 4.5 contains information that may simply be checked, if present in an intervention program. It also allows program staff, or an interviewer, to add activities in each major category. This instrument might be completed as a mail survey. It has also been used during interviews with intervention program staff.

The items contained in Figure 4.5 are meant to be illustrative rather than exhaustive. States and local coalitions of early intervention agencies will want to add and delete items to best describe the programs in their areas.

We suggest that a separate instrument be used to identify early intervention experts for a central directory. The instrument contained in Figure 4.6 is useful for this purpose. This instrument can be completed in less than 5 minutes, and it can be used to both develop and update a central directory.

Linkages with Other Instruments

The two instruments that are shown in figures 4.5 and 4.6 can be used together to build a statewide central directory. Services offered by early intervention programs can be presented for a geographic area along with an identification of expert personnel in those programs and in those geographic areas.

Suggestions for Data Coding and Analysis

Initial coding of data on early intervention programs and experts will be time consuming unless such information exists for other purposes. Once a central

Figure 4.5
EARLY INTERVENTION PROGRAM DESCRIPTION

Instructions. The purpose of this instrument is to describe in a quick fashion the services provided by early intervention programs operating in the state. These programs serve infants and toddlers and their families. Please check below the activities (as they apply to infants and toddlers and families) in which your program is engaged.

Program Title: _____

Program Address: _____

Person Completing This Description: _____

Telephone During Day: (_____) _____
                  Area   Number

Date of Submission: _____ / _____ / _____

Check if submission is an update: _____

Geographic Area Served by Program: _____

Please check below the activities conducted by your early intervention program. If you have specific information to share about any of those activities, please do so in the Comments column below.

Comments

Child Find/Screening

1. _____ Advertisement. _____

2. _____ Screening clinics. _____

3. _____ Home visit by public health nurse. _____

4. _____ Well baby clinic. _____

5. _____ Other: _____

6. _____ Other: _____

7. _____ Other: _____

Figure 4.5 (Continued)

Comments

Screening and Diagnostic Services

1. _____ Screening of risk factors.

2. _____ Screening of infant and toddler performances.

3. _____ Multidisciplinary diagnostic assessment of developmental delay.

4. _____ Other: _____

5. _____ Other: _____

6. _____ Other: _____

Referral Services

1. _____ Infants and families are referred to another agency.

2. _____ Infant and family participation in another agency is tracked through organized referral system.

3. _____ Infants and families are accepted on a referral basis from other agencies.

4. _____ A procedure is employed to determine how long after referral *to* another agency services are provided.

5. _____ A procedure is employed to determine how long after referral *from* another agency services are provided.

6. _____ Other: _____

Figure 4.5 (Continued)

Comments

Referral Services (Continued)

7. ____ Other: _____

8. ____ Other: _____

Programmatic Assessment as a Part of Intervention

1. ____ Ongoing developmental monitoring of children not in program but being monitored. _____

2. ____ Ongoing developmental monitoring of children in program. _____

3. ____ Other: _____

4. ____ Other: _____

5. ____ Other: _____

Service Delivery Programs

1. ____ Home visits. _____

2. ____ Center-based services/child alone. _____

3. ____ Center-based services/child and family alone. _____

4. ____ Center-based services/individual parents (alone). _____

5. ____ Visits to other child care programs. _____

Figure 4.5 (Continued)

Comments

Service Delivery Programs (Continued)

6. ____ Specialized services to particular groups of parents (e.g., MR parents).

7. ____ Center-based services to all parents in groups.

8. ____ Transitional programming for children moving to preschool programs.

9. ____ Other: _____

10. ____ Other: _____

11. ____ Other: _____

Case Management

1. ____ Professional case manager (i.e., person whose primary responsibilities are case management).

2. ____ One member of interdisciplinary team serves as case manager.

3. ____ Entire team acts as case managers.

4. ____ Parents are own case managers.

5. ____ Other: _____

Figure 4.5 (Continued)

Comments

Training

1. _____ Train staff at day care centers for normally developing children in which developmentally delayed or at-risk children are enrolled. _____

2. _____ Train pediatricians. _____

3. _____ Train staff in other programs serving developmentally delayed, handicapped, or at-risk children but not receiving 99-457 funds. _____

4. _____ Other: _____

5. _____ Other: _____

6. _____ Other: _____

Figure 4.6
IDENTIFYING EARLY INTERVENTION RESOURCES

Instructions. This form is to be used to identify *individuals* who have expertise in one or more areas of early intervention for handicapped infants and toddlers (children aged birth through 2 years, inclusive, who are handicapped, developmentally delayed, or at risk for developmental delay). Individuals contributing to this request for information will become a part of a statewide central directory of early childhood experts. This directory will be made available to early intervention programs throughout the state and updated regularly. Individual contributing to this central directory are under no obligation to perform services for the state or for any specific early intervention program. Any assistance provided by experts (in the central directory) to early intervention programs is based upon common agreements of services and fees between the experts and the staff of the early intervention programs.

1. Date of completion of this form: _____ / _____ / _____

   Is this form an update of previous information? Yes _____ No _____

2. Name: _____

3. Do you currently work for any early intervention program? Yes _____ No _____

   If so, what is the name of that program? _____

   address of that program? _____

   If so, what percentage of full-time equivalent (37–40 hrs./week) do you work? _____ % of FTE

4. Preferred mailing address: _____ _____ _____ _____
                               Number and Street   City   State   Zip

   Telephone number (_____) _____ Preferred time for telephone? _____
                     Area   Number

5. What title best describes your position? _____

6. Please check below the area(s) of early intervention activity in which you have expertise.

Figure 4.6 (Continued)

ASSESSMENT OF INFANTS AND TODDLERS

_____ Physical assessment

_____ Cognitive assessment

_____ Language/communication assessment

_____ Self-help assessment

_____ Psychosocial assessment

_____ Other (or more specific area of assessment expertise)

_____ Please explain _____

INTERVENTION WITH INFANTS AND TODDLERS

_____ Physical therapy

_____ Occupational therapy

_____ Speech/language therapy

_____ Other therapy (Please explain): _____

_____ Planning educational programs

_____ Delivering educational programs

ASSESSMENT OF FAMILIES

_____ Assessing family knowledge of child development

_____ Assessing family involvement in early intervention

Figure 4.6 (Continued)

_____ Assessing family needs for financial assistance

_____ Assessing family needs for shelter/food

_____ Assessing family needs related to medical/nutritional care

_____ Assessing family educational/job training needs

_____ Assessing family communication needs

_____ Assessing other family needs (Please explain): _____

INTERVENTION WITH FAMILIES

_____ Planning family intervention

_____ Delivering family intervention

Specific areas of family intervention: _____

TRAINING OF EARLY INTERVENTION PERSONNEL

_____ Training in assessment of infants and toddlers

Specific type of assessment training: _____

_____ Training in assessment of families

Specific type of assessment training: _____

_____ Training in areas of early intervention with infants and toddlers

Specific areas of training: _____

Figure 4.6 (Continued)

___ Training in areas of family intervention

___ Specific areas of training: _____

RESEARCH WITH INFANTS AND TODDLERS AND FAMILIES

___ Research with infants and toddlers

Brief description of research focus: _____

___ Research with families

Brief description of research focus: _____

7. Please indicate the geographic area(s) of the state in which you would consider sharing your early intervention expertise.

_____

8. If there is any further information to share regarding your early intervention expertise, please do so in the following space:

_____

_____

_____

_____

_____

_____

_____

directory has been established, however, subsequent data entry will consist primarily of updates, although new programs may become established and persons with expertise in early intervention may come into (or leave) the state.

Component 8: Personnel Development Training

The Required Component

A comprehensive system of early intervention must contain a comprehensive system of personnel development. The system must include training of public and private service providers, primary referral sources, and persons who will provide services after receiving such training.

Background

The personnel development component required by P.L. 99-457 is considered by its congressional authors to be one of the most important in the entire early intervention system. According to the proposed regulations (see Chapter 2), the personnel development system must include both preservice and inservice training. Such training is to be conducted on an interdisciplinary basis, to the extent appropriate. This concept of preservice *and* inservice training is a recognition that training must occur prior to and after employment, and retraining is likely to be necessary if new standards are established.

Many states have established personnel development systems under the previously existing Part B of the Education of All Handicapped Children Act (P.L. 94-142) for preschool children. Such existing systems may satisfy the required Part H Personnel Development Component, provided that they are broad enough to include the greater diversity of professionals who are working with infants and toddlers.

Instrumentation

The proposed regulations guiding development of this component (see Chapter 2) indicate that the personnel development system that must be created, or modified, under Part H of P.L. 99-457 must include a list showing each profession or discipline in which personnel are providing early intervention services. To assist in generating such information, we have designed a form (Figure 4.7), the Early Intervention Personnel Development Form, that is a modification of the forms used to develop the central directory required in the previous component.

Figure 4.7
EARLY INTERVENTION PERSONNEL DEVELOPMENT FORM

Instructions. This instrument is to be used to identify agencies and institutions providing training in areas of early intervention. The training provided by these agencies and institutions may be offered on a preservice or an inservice basis. Information gathered from this form may become part of a statewide central directory of early intervention resources.

1. Date of completion of this form: _____ / _____ / _____

   Is this form an update of previous information? Yes _____ No _____

2. Name of person with primary responsibility for completion of this form: _____

   Title: _____

3. Institution's mailing address: _____

   Number and Street   City   State   Zip

   Institution's location (if different): _____

   Number and Street   City   State   Zip

   Telephone number (_____) _____

   Area   Number   Preferred time for telephone

4. Please check the area(s) of early intervention activity in which your agency or institution provides training. Also, please check if the training provided at your institution is best described as preservice (entry level) or inservice (with practicing professionals who have already completed entry level training).

Figure 4.7 (Continued)

ASSESSMENT OF INFANTS AND TODDLERS

Preservice (Entry Level)	Inservice (Post-Entry Level)	
___	___	Physical assessment
___	___	Cognitive assessment
___	___	Language/communication assessment
___	___	Self-held assessment
___	___	Psychosocial assessment
___	___	Other (or more specific area of assessment expertise)
		Please explain: _____

INTERVENTION WITH INFANTS AND TODDLERS

___	___	Physical therapy
___	___	Occupational therapy
___	___	Speech/language therapy
___	___	Other therapy (Please explain): _____
___		Planning educational programs
___		Delivering educational programs

Figure 4.7 (Continued)

ASSESSMENT OF FAMILIES

Preservice (Entry Level)	Inservice (Post-Entry Level)	
____	____	Assessing family knowledge of child development
____	____	Assessing family involvement in early intervention
____	____	Assessing family needs for financial assistance
____	____	Assessing family needs for shelter/food
____	____	Assessing family needs related to medical/nutritional care
____	____	Assessing family educational/job training needs
____	____	Assessing family communication needs
____	____	Assessing other family needs (Please explain): _____

INTERVENTION WITH FAMILIES

____	____	Planning family intervention
____	____	Delivering family intervention

Specific areas of family intervention: _____

_____

_____

_____

Figure 4.7 (Continued)

TRAINING OF EARLY INTERVENTION PERSONNEL

Preservice (Entry Level)	Inservice (Post-Entry Level)	
_____	_____	Training in assessment of infants and toddlers
		Specific type of assessment training: _____
_____	_____	Training in assessment of families
		Specific type of assessment training: _____
_____	_____	Training in areas of early intervention with infants and toddlers
		Specific areas of training: _____
_____	_____	Training in areas of family intervention:
		Specific areas of training: _____

RESEARCH WITH INFANTS AND TODDLERS AND FAMILIES

_____	_____	Research with infants and toddlers
		Brief description of research focus: _____
_____	_____	Research with families
		Brief description of research focus: _____

Figure 4.7 (Continued)

5. If there are any geographic constraints upon your training capabilities, please indicate them:

6. If there is any further information to share regarding your training capabilities in early intervention, please do so in the following spaces:

_____

_____

_____

_____

_____

_____

_____

_____

_____

_____

_____

_____

_____

_____

_____

Linkages with Other Instruments

The Early Intervention Personnel Development Form is designed to be complementary to the two instruments suggested for the previous component. Listing of personnel development resources could, if desired, become a part of a regularly published central directory.

Suggestions for Data Coding and Analysis

The information generated by the Early Intervention Personnel Development Form can be used to complete Table 5 of the federal reporting requirements (OSEP Memorandum, 1988), which is an identification of needs in the statewide early intervention system. Personnel needs might be geographic areas lacking training or retraining capabilities, or they might indicate professions or disciplines in which training is not based on the highest requirements established in the state.

Component 9: Lead Agency Authority

The Required Component

We have mentioned several times that P.L. 99-457 mandates a single line of responsibility in a lead agency designated or established by the governor for carrying out numerous administrative and fiscal functions. A key function vested in the lead agency is the monitoring of programs and activities to ensure compliance with federal law and regulation.

Background

P.L. 99-457 represents an attempt to mandate interagency collaboration for purposes of ensuring continuous, high-quality intervention for handicapped infants and toddlers. Such a mandate represents a bold and perhaps idealistic effort to bring together agencies that have already defined independent spheres of interest and activity (Sheehan & Sites, in press). The idealism evident in this law is tempered by a pragmatic awareness that there must be a single line of authority from the federal government to the state and downward to local early intervention agencies.

We describe in Chapter 1 the various ways in which states have designated lead agencies. In some states, (e.g., Indiana), the state Department of Mental Health is the designated lead agency. Elsewhere (e.g., Ohio) the designated lead agency is the Department of Health. A minority of states have designated the state Department of Education, and a majority of states have involved health-related agencies as their designated lead agency.

The role of the designated lead agency in monitoring and centralized data collection cannot be overemphasized. In instances where a new agency has been formed to be the lead agency, monitoring and review procedures and data collection systems must be newly created. These tasks are not much easier for lead agencies operating in established settings, because existing systems must be modified to incorporate procedures and systems from collaborating agencies. We recognize that modification of existing systems can be as difficult, or more difficult, than creation of new systems. This text is written in an effort to ease such difficulties.

Our contacts, to date, with lead agency staff have indicated remarkable fluidity in design and implementation of comprehensive data collection systems. States seem aware that federal reporting requirements may change, and they seem determined to design data collection systems that are of true benefit in ensuring high-quality early intervention. This positive attitude of lead agency staff who are implementing the infant/toddler component of P.L. 99-457 is a good model for any agencies that assume responsibility for a complex early intervention system. A recognition that high-quality early intervention mandates interagency functioning is a first step in the design of a comprehensive early intervention system. This recognition is evident in the federal, state, and local early childhood providers with whom we have worked.

Instrumentation

No instrumentation is necessary to document the existence of this component. We do anticipate that federal and state policymakers will want to evaluate the functioning of lead agencies, and this will necessitate the development of appropriate instruments. Such evaluations are likely to be several years away and beyond the scope of this text.

Component 10: Local Service Provider Contracts

The Required Component

The 10th component of the mandated state system for early intervention is the existence of a policy pertaining to the contracting or making of other arrangements with service providers in a state to provide early intervention services consistent with P.L. 99-457. This component is a recognition that a state-designated lead agency must establish procedures by which early childhood providers from other state agencies or from private entities are included in the statewide, comprehensive early intervention system.

Background

The language and intent of P.L. 99-457 are very clear in pointing out that early intervention for infants and toddlers requires coordination of both new and existing service providers. The comprehensive early intervention system resulting from P.L. 99-457 differs from programs that have existed longer (e.g., Head Start) in that existing service providers *must* be made a part of the new comprehensive system. When Head Start (and many other early education programs) was established, a totally new system was created and put in place. New staff were hired, facilities were purchased or leased, and a highly centralized curriculum was disseminated across the country. The total funding allocation for P.L. 99-457, though significant for early intervention, is only a minute fraction of that of Head Start. Although there are many handicapped infants and toddlers in this country, there are far fewer such children than there are preschoolers eligible for a program such as Head Start. The political climate surrounding social programs has shifted; no longer do we focus our sole attention on nationally based large-scale, single-system approaches. Public Law 99-457 represents one aspect of this change.

The development of more state-specific systems, involving many agencies, increases the need for careful monitoring of the contracts and subcontracts of early childhood service providers. State-designated lead agencies are responsible for ensuring that early intervention service providers are properly developing and implementing IFSPs for handicapped infants and toddlers and their families. Early intervention services being delivered must be timely, and consistent with federal, state, and local law and regulation. Local service providers must agree to provide reliable and valid data through appropriate channels to state-designated lead agencies.

Instrumentation

The instruments presented in this text can be used with any contracted early childhood provider, as all such contracts must be consistent with P.L. 99-457. State-designated lead agencies will need to evaluate performance occurring under those contracts; however, such evaluation is beyond the scope of this text.

Component 11: Reimbursement Provisions

The Required Component

The comprehensive early intervention system must also include a procedure for timely reimbursement of funds.

Background

The comments found in House Report 99-860 (see Chapter 2 for discussion of this report) are simply a restatement of this component. Obviously, Congress was well aware that participants in a statewide, comprehensive early intervention system must receive timely reimbursement of funds to continue delivering intervention services. The fact that state-designated lead agencies must ensure such timeliness is a reflection of the priority evident in P.L. 99-457 for rapid onset of early intervention. Administrative logjams, including delays in funding, should not be a part of the new statewide early intervention system.

This required component, for timely reimbursement of funds, also reflects the recognition that many statewide, comprehensive early intervention systems will include relatively small, private early intervention service providers. Such providers do not have sufficient cash flow (or credit capabilities) to wait 6 to 12 months for reimbursement of expenses for early intervention services.

Instrumentation

We do not suggest instrumentation in this area. State lead agencies are responsible to demonstrate timely reimbursement of funds to collaborating state agencies and to local service providers. Existing auditing procedures must be made consistent with state assurances of such timeliness, and state-designated lead agencies are subject to administrative appeal if such timeliness cannot be demonstrated.

Component 12: Procedural Safeguards

The Required Component

The comprehensive early intervention systems created under P.L. 99-457 must have a number of mandated procedural safeguards. These safeguards –

timely administrative resolution of complaints, confidentiality, access to records by parents, and due process procedures – are all designed to protect the rights of children and families, while ensuring that early intervention services are uninterrupted during administrative proceedings.

Background

The authors of P.L. 99-457 were well aware of the need for procedural safeguards to (a) protect the rights of handicapped infants and toddlers and their families and (b) ensure that services are being delivered to children with demonstrated eligibility. The litigation leading up to the passage of P.L. 94-142 and the subsequent appeals suggested that legislation supporting special educational and related services will, at times, be the subject of legal actions.

The recognition of possible legal action in early intervention cases was also tempered by the realization that court actions can be lengthy, and infant and toddler development proceeds on a rapid course. None of the congressional authors of P.L. 99-457 wanted infants and toddlers to become victims of time in the appeals process.

To ensure the existence and functioning of procedural safeguards, agencies must first demonstrate that such safeguards exist. Are records being maintained in a confidential fashion? Do procedures exist to appoint an individual (who is not an employee of the state agency providing services) to act as surrogate for parents when the parents or guardian are unknown? Is a time line established for provision of written notice to parents, or guardian, or designated surrogate whenever a service provider proposes a change in eligibility status of an infant or toddler? The proposed regulations for P.L. 99-457 (see Chapter 2) have suggested that *timely* is a term that translates to 30 days or less. Evaluations of infants and families are expected to be completed within 30 calendar days after referral.

The second responsibility that agencies have with regard to procedural safeguards is to ensure that such safeguards are clearly and fully communicated to parents and guardians in the native language of the affected families. The concern here is that all participants in the comprehensive early intervention system must be aware of their rights and responsibilities in that system.

The third responsibility of agencies with regard to procedural responsibilities is to regularly monitor the implementation of those services. Are children continuing to receive early intervention services during the course of any proceeding or complaint action? Exactly how much time is passing from notification of a complaint to resolution of such concerns? How much time is given to parents to respond to written notifications of a change in a child's eligibility status?

These three responsibilities – ensuring existence of procedural safeguards, communicating existing of such safeguards, and monitoring functioning of procedural safeguards – should be familiar to administrators and staff in early intervention agencies. When they are unfamiliar, the responsibilities should be a required component of employee training and inservice.

Instrumentation

No instruments have been developed for this component of P.L. 99-457. In most agencies, existing procedures for ensuring due process will, with slight modifications, suffice to monitor the existence and functioning of this component of a comprehensive early intervention system. The authors of P.L. 99-457 permit states to adopt the full set of procedural safeguards that currently exist in support of Part B of the Education of All Handicapped Children Act (P.L. 94-142). Alternatively, states may modify existing procedural safeguards or develop new procedures, as long as any new or modified procedures are consistent with the requirements of P.L. 99-457.

Component 13: Personnel Standards

The Required Component

Public Law 99-457 mandates the creation or adoption of personnel standards to ensure that staff participating in the comprehensive early intervention system are appropriately and adequately prepared and trained. This component most significantly affects states that have not yet established personnel standards for early childhood special educators, as such standards are now mandated under P.L. 99-457.

Background

The need for personnel standards for early intervention specialists is dramatic. Meisels, Harbin, Modigliana, and Olson (1988) recently surveyed all states in the country and discovered that one quarter of those states have no certification for teachers of handicapped children, aged birth through 6 years. Further, 69% of the states lack sufficient training programs to prepare needed professionals. They report: "An alarming shortage of trained early childhood special educators, and physical, occupational, and speech therapists was identified – this shortage projected to continue until the end of this decade" (p. 16).

The reasons for the current shortage of trained early intervention personnel are clear from the comments made in Chapter 1 of this text. Legislation passed prior to P.L. 99-457 was permissive, and underfunded. Preschoolers, infants, and toddlers and their families have not been primary targets for intervention efforts in most statewide education systems. The shortage of trained personnel is simply a reflection of the fact that few employment opportunities were available for persons wanting to work with young handicapped children and their families. This shortage can and will change in response to P.L. 99-457.

Federal reporting requirements currently indicate that state-designated lead agencies must annually report the number of staff (in full-time equivalents) working in each state by category of job (OSEP Memorandum, 1988). Lead agencies must also report the number of staff (in full-time equivalents) needed to maintain the full educational opportunity goal to provide early intervention services for handicapped infants and toddlers. The categories established for this reporting are built into the instrument shown in Figure 4.8.

Instrumentation

State-specific instruments are likely to be developed as states establish (and review) personnel standards for the many disciplines found in early intervention settings. The Early Intervention Staff Characteristics Form shown in Figure 4.8 represents a generic method for gathering data on the educational and experiential background of intervention project staff. Figure 4.8 also can be used to gather data that could be reported for federal reporting requirements (on Table 3 of OSEP Memorandum, 1988).

Linkages with Other Instruments

The Early Intervention Staff Characteristics Form has been designed in a format similar to other instruments in this text, employing the same confidentiality options evident in those instruments. Staff members are to be assigned a consistent code, and reporting may, at option of an intervention project (or a lead agency), include staff members' names.

Suggestions for Data Coding and Analysis

For federal reporting purposes, data analysis can simply be a count, by occupational category, of the number of personnel indicated in items 2 and 3 of the Early Intervention Staff Characteristics Form. This form has also proven useful for describing the demographic characteristics of staff employed with a comprehensive early intervention system (e.g., number of years experience of staff with instructional responsibilities).

Figure 4.8
EARLY INTERVENTION STAFF CHARACTERISTICS FORM

Instructions. The purpose of this instrument is to gather data on the characteristics of staff members in an early intervention program. Staff members' names may, at the discretion of the early intervention program staff, be included in this analysis. In the event that a staff member's name is included in the analysis, program staff *must* still assign a unique identifier number to each child being served by the program. If an early intervention program chooses to only record identification numbers in the analysis, the program staff assume responsibility for maintaining a master record of staff members' identifies and their respective identification numbers. In general, staff characteristics are to be described for **every staff member who has direct contact or administrative responsibility for infants and toddlers in an agency or a contracted program.**

Program Title: _____

Program Address: _____

Person Submitting This Analysis: _____

Telephone During Day: (_____) _____
              Area   Number

Date Submitted: _____ / _____ / _____

Part A

1. Please indicate the number of staff whose sole responsibility for the early intervention program is administrative in nature:

_____ Staff Administrators

2. Please indicate the number of staff whose sole responsibility for the early intervention program is instructional or supportive services (including assessment, counseling, educational, etc.):

_____ Staff Interventionists

3. Please indicate the number of staff who have a combined administrative and instructional/supportive service role in the early intervention program:

_____ Staff with combined roles

Figure 4.8 (Continued)

Part B

Provide the following information for every staff member included in Part A.

1. Staff member's name: _____ ID: _____

2. Position title (check one)

____ Special educator

____ Speech and language pathologist

____ Audiologist

____ Occupational therapist

____ Physical therapist

____ Psychologist

____ Social worker

____ Nurse

____ Nutritionist

____ Other professional staff (describe): _____

a. Does a job description exist for this position? ____ Yes ____ No

b. If so, attach a copy of the job description to this instrument.

3. Percent of a full-time equivalence worked (37–40 hrs. per week): ____ % FTE

4. Gender: ____ Male ____ Female

Figure 4.8 (Continued)

5. Years experience working with infants with handicaps (or at risk) ———— Years

6. Total years of experience working with special education populations: ———— Years

7. Total years of experience working in current position: ———— Years

8. Educational preparation (Please check and specify *all* that apply):

a. ———— High school graduate

b. ———— Community college graduate (Specify major): ————————————————

c. ———— Bachelor's degree (Specify major): ————————————————

d. ———— Bachelor's plus some graduate hours (Specify major): ————————————————

e. ———— Master's degree (Specify major): ————————————————

f. ———— Graduate hours past the master's degree (specify area of additional coursework): ————

g. ———— EdS (Specify major): ————————————————

h. ———— Doctoral degree (PhD, EdD, MD) (Specify major): ————————————————

i. ———— Other (describe) ————————————————

9. Type of certification: ————————————————

State: ———— Classification: ————

10. Please briefly describe your job responsibilities: ————————————————

——

Component 14: A System for Compiling Data

The Required Component

The final component of a comprehensive early intervention system required by P.L. 99-457 is a system for compiling data on the numbers of handicapped infants and toddlers and their families in need of services as well as data describing services delivered to children by that system.

Background

The early intervention system supported by P.L. 99-457 represents the most recent development in our society's efforts to promote early childhood growth and development. The cost of such an effort, $67 million for fiscal year 1988 in federal funds alone, is high. The challenge facing early intervention specialists is great. The data system required by P.L. 99-457 represents an effort to monitor the success of this effort.

Instrumentation

The eight instruments discussed thus far in this book can be made an integral part of a data management system. The instruments are as follows:

1. Early Intervention Services Eligibility Record (Component 1, Figure 4.1): useful for completing Table 1 of Federal Report (OSEP Memorandum, 1988).

2. Checklist for Early Intervention Timetables (Component 2, Figure 4.2): useful for completing Table 5 of Federal Report (OSEP Memorandum, 1988).

3. Analysis of Individualized Family Service Plans (Components 3 & 4, Figure 4.3): useful for completing Table 2 of Federal Report (OSEP Memorandum, 1988).

4. Individualized Family Service Plan (IFSP) Form (Components 3 & 4, Figure 4.4): useful for completing Table 2 of Federal Report (OSEP Memorandum, 1988).

5. Early Intervention Program Description (Component 7, Figure 4.5).

6. Identifying Early Intervention Resources (Component 7, Figure 4.6).

7. Early Intervention Personnel Development Form (Component 8, Figure 4.7): useful for completing Table 5 of Federal Report (OSEP Memorandum, 1988).

8. Early Intervention Staff Characteristics Form (Component 13, Figure 4.8): useful for completing Table 3 of Federal Report (OSEP Memorandum, 1988).

As noted above, several of these instruments are useful for currently known federal reporting purposes (OSEP Memorandum, 1988). There is still a need, however, for an instrument designed to collect information on the type, frequency, duration, and cost of intervention services provided to infants and toddlers and their families under P.L. 99-457. There is also a need to gather information on the need of improvement in the early intervention system as seen by participants in that system. For these purposes, a multipart instrument entitled the Early Intervention Services Report was designed (Figure 4.9). Two specific parts of this instrument, Part L and Part M, were developed to correspond exactly to tables 4 and 5, respectively, of federal reporting form OSEP Memorandum (1988). Remaining parts of the instrument provide data useful for reporting on Table 2 of this federal report.

As mentioned previously, instruments presented in this book are designed to be illustrative rather than exhaustive. State-designated lead agencies and local early intervention agencies may need to modify all or parts of Figure 4.9 to make it applicable to their situation.

Linkages with Other Instruments

The Early Intervention Services Report (Figure 4.9) has been designed in a format similar to the other instruments in this book. Common terminology has been used in all instruments, and coding systems have been kept consistent for all the data collection tools presented in this chapter.

State-designated lead agencies and local early intervention agencies choosing to modify the Early Intervention Services Report (Figure 4.9) should be careful to modify all selected instruments in a similar fashion. We repeat our previous comment that early intervention personnel are reluctant (at best) to collect data that are used primarily for reporting purposes; however, consistency of terminology and formating help to ensure greater support from those early intervention specialists who are asked to present such data.

Suggestions for Data Coding and Analysis

The very length of Figure 4.9 almost mandates some form of computerized data entry. Once again, to reduce coding errors, we have used data-based

Figure 4.9
EARLY INTERVENTION SERVICES REPORT

Contents

Definitions
Part A   Documenting services provided to infants and toddlers and families
Part B   Summarizing center-based instructional schedules
Part C   Summarizing home-based service schedules
Part D   Summarizing individual therapy schedules
Part E   Summarizing off-site monitoring service schedules
Part F   Documenting child-find activities
Part G   Summarizing screening and diagnostic services to infants and toddlers and families
Part H   Documenting external activities for infants and toddlers and families
Part I   Documenting family training and counseling services
Part J   Describing training and technical assistance to other providers
Part K   Describing waiting lists and waiting list activities
Part L   Describing funding sources of early intervention
Part M   Describing early intervention needs

Program Title: _____ ID: _____

Program Address: _____

Person Submitting This Analysis: _____

Telephone During Day: (_____) _____
                         Area   Number

Date Submitted: _____ / _____ / _____

Figure 4.9 (Continued)

IDENTIFYING INDIVIDUAL DEVELOPMENTALLY DELAYED, HANDICAPPED, AND AT-RISK INFANTS AND TODDLERS

This report requests information on the intervention activities of specific infants and toddlers and their families (see Part A). The report format permits a program to record children's names, birth dates, and identification numbers. If a program is able to record children's names in this report, the program *must* also record children's birth dates and identification numbers. Any children without identification numbers must be provided such a number. If an early intervention program is not permitted to indicate children's identity by name, the program *must* report children's birth dates and identification numbers. While families are an integral component of a comprehensive early intervention system, we leave it up to individual states or local service providers to decide whether to assign each family a unique identifying code number. If an early intervention program decides to not assign such a number, services to families information can be recorded in the identification code of a child. If an early intervention program (or state request) suggests the need for a unique family identifier, a 2- or 3-digit identifying number could be used with an additional digit (i.e., 1 or 2) to refer to particular children in that family who are participating in the early intervention system.

PROVIDING SUMMARY INFORMATION

In addition to providing information about the intervention activities of specifically identified infants, toddlers, and families, program staff are also asked to summarize that information (on appropriate forms) in such a way that patterns and overall scope of intervention services are revealed (Parts B, C, D, E, F, G, H, I, J, K, L, and M).

DEFINING CENTER-BASED PROGRAM

These are educational and diagnostic services provided by the early intervention program or a contracted program to infants and toddlers and their families who are in center-based settings. The unit of activity that should be reflected in the data below is the center-based program that is serving infants and toddlers or that is capable of serving infants and toddlers. In general, this will represent the entire infant/toddler center-based program of an applicant or a contracting program. *Note:* This category of service is *not* to be used for screening or diagnostic assessment of children prior to their admittance to an intervention program. Such activity is recorded as a separate activity entitled "Screening and Diagnostic Services."

DEFINING HOME-BASED PROGRAM

These are educational and diagnostic services provided by the early intervention program or a contracting program in the home (or homelike setting) of an infant or toddler. Such services are most often provided in the specific home of a child, but they may also be provided in the home of a relative, baby-sitter, or friend or in a day-care home. *Note:* This category of services is *not* used for therapy delivered in a home by a certified therapist. For such therapy services, use the next category entitled "Individual Therapy Services."

Figure 4.9 (Continued)

DEFINING INDIVIDUAL THERAPY SERVICES

These are services provided by a certified therapist (e.g., speech therapist, occupational therapist, physical therapist) to a specific infant or toddler. Such services may be provided on a "pull-out basis" in a location away from other children, or they may be provided in a center-based setting, in a child's home, or in a day-care home.

DEFINING OFF-SITE MONITORING SERVICES

These are brief educational and diagnostic services provided by the early intervention program or a contracting program to an infant or toddler in a mainstream center-based program that is *not* the program of the early intervention program or the contracting program. These services are best represented by the program that facilitates a child being served in another mainstream setting by agreeing to periodically monitor that child's progress in the mainstream setting.

DEFINING CHILD-FIND ACTIVITIES

These are activities designed to locate infants and toddlers who should be screened and assessed to determine their eligibility for services. Child-find activities will vary in type from development and dissemination of promotional materials, to media releases, to public forums.

DEFINING SCREENING AND DIAGNOSTIC SERVICES

These are services provided to infants and toddlers and their families prior to or once enrolled in an early intervention program. Such children may already be enrolled in a program, they may eventually become enrolled in a program, they may be referred elsewhere for services, or they may be reassessed at some later time.

DEFINING AUDIOLOGICAL SERVICES

These are services designed to determine the range, nature, and degree of hearing loss. They are also services providing habilitative activities as well as assessment of a child's need for amplification.

DEFINING MEDICAL SERVICES

These are medical activities conducted only for diagnostic or evaluation purposes.

Figure 4.9 (Continued)

DEFINING HEALTH SERVICES

These are health-related activities necessary to enable a child to benefit from early intervention services (e.g., catheterization). This category of services cannot be used to indicate services that are surgical or purely medical in nature (e.g., cleft palate surgery, management of cystic fibrosis, and shunting of hydrocephalus).

DEFINING EXTERNAL REFERRALS

Referrals link children suspected of (or diagnosed as) having handicapping conditions, development delays, or risk conditions to agencies and providers *other than* the referring program. The key characteristic of such referrals is that a contact is made by one program to link a child and his or her family with *another* program.

DEFINING FAMILY TRAINING AND COUNSELING

Family training and counseling includes any formal educational or counseling effort directed at one or more parents whose infant or toddler is enrolled in a program. The two defining criteria for this activity include the "formal" nature of the training (i.e., not training occurring during a casual conversation between a staff member and a parent) and the fact that the child must be enrolled in the program.

DEFINING TRAINING AND TECHNICAL ASSISTANCE TO OTHER PROVIDERS

These are training and technical assistance efforts directed toward early childhood personnel who may be caring for or working with infants and toddlers during portions of the day when those children are not in formal intervention programs. This category of service is also represented by training or technical assistance directed toward child care providers who may not be working specifically with infants and toddlers enrolled in intervention programs but may be working with other young children.

DEFINING WAITING LISTS AND WAITING LIST ACTIVITIES

Waiting lists represent a listing of names, addresses, and birth dates of infants or toddlers who qualify for services but are not yet receiving those services due to a program's operating at full capacity or a program's inability to meet the specific needs of a child. A child who qualifies for services but has not yet begun to receive them due to factors beyond a program's control (e.g., childhood illness) is not considered to be on a waiting list. Waiting list activities include those intervention efforts (typically continued monitoring or brief home visiting) directed at children on waiting lists.

Figure 4.9 (Continued)

PART A
DOCUMENTING SERVICES PROVIDED TO INFANTS AND TODDLERS AND FAMILIES

Reporting Period: from ____ / ____ / ____ to ____ / ____ / ____

Instructions. On this form, report only the services provided to infants and toddlers who are declared to be eligible for services under P.L. 99-457 eligibility criteria.

NAME	BIRTH DATE	ID	CENTER-BASED HOURS	HOME-BASED HOURS	HOURS	THERAPY TYPE* (check) OT PT ST	OTHER (specify)	OFF-SITE MONITORING VISITS
____	__/__/__	____	____	____	____	__ __ __	____	____
____	__/__/__	____	____	____	____	__ __ __	____	____
____	__/__/__	____	____	____	____	__ __ __	____	____
____	__/__/__	____	____	____	____	__ __ __	____	____
____	__/__/__	____	____	____	____	__ __ __	____	____
____	__/__/__	____	____	____	____	__ __ __	____	____
____	__/__/__	____	____	____	____	__ __ __	____	____

*OT = occupational therapy; PT = physical therapy; ST = speech therapy.

CONTINUE THIS PAGE AS NECESSARY

Figure 4.9 (Continued)

PART B

SUMMARIZING CENTER-BASED INSTRUCTIONAL SCHEDULES

Instructions. List below the number of infants and toddlers participating in center-based early intervention programs and the number of hours in which groups of children participate. Be as specific as possible in describing the variations of center-based instructional schedules. Do *not*, however, differentiate between schedules of children based upon unanticipated absences of children. (That is, a child who normally attends a program 20 hours per week but was sick 1 day would still be recorded within the group that attends 20 hours per week.)

CHILDREN	SCHEDULES	TOTAL SERVICES	SERVICE PROVIDER
Column A	Column B	Multiply Column A × B	Column C
No. 99-457 Eligible Children	No. Hours/ Week	No. Hours/ Service/Week	Agency Providing Service
_____	_____	_____	_____
_____	_____	_____	_____
_____	_____	_____	_____
_____	_____	_____	_____
_____	_____	_____	_____
_____	_____	_____	_____
_____	_____	_____	_____
			_____

CONTINUE THIS PAGE AS NECESSARY

Figure 4.9 (Continued)

PART C
SUMMARIZING HOME-BASED SERVICE SCHEDULES

Instructions. List below the number of infants and toddlers and families receiving home-based educational and diagnostic services and the number of hours of service received by various groups of children. Do *not* differentiate between schedules of home-based services that may have been affected by children's short-term illness or absence. *Note:* This category of services is *not* used for therapy delivered in a home by a certified therapist. For such therapy services, use the next category entitled "Individual Therapy Services."

CHILDREN	SCHEDULES		TOTAL SERVICES
Column A	Column B	Column C	Multiply Column A × B × C
No. 99-457 Eligible Children	No. Minutes/ Visit	No. Visits/ Month	No. Minutes/ Service/Month
_____	_____	_____	_____
_____	_____	_____	_____
_____	_____	_____	_____
_____	_____	_____	_____
_____	_____	_____	_____
_____	_____	_____	_____
_____	_____	_____	_____
_____	_____	_____	_____

CONTINUE THIS PAGE AS NECESSARY

Figure 4.9 (Continued)

PART D
SUMMARIZING INDIVIDUAL THERAPY SCHEDULES

Instructions: List below the number of infants and toddlers receiving individual therapy services from a certified therapist. Note the number of hours of therapy per month received by children and differentiate this information by type of therapy. Do *not* differentiate between schedules of therapy services that may have been affected by children's short-term illness or absence. *Note:* Therapy may have been delivered on a "pull-out basis" in a location away from other children or it may be provided in a center-based setting, in a child's home, or in a day-care home. Two criteria that must be met in this category are that the therapy must have been provided by a certified therapist and the therapy must have been provided to children on an individual basis.

CHILDREN	MINUTES	SESSIONS	THERAPY TYPE		
Column A	Column B	Column C	Type of Therapy*		
			ST	OT	PT	OTHER
No. 99-457 Eligible Children	No. Minutes/ Therapy/Session	No. Therapy Session/Month	(check one)		
____	____	____	___	___	___	___
____	____	____	___	___	___	___
____	____	____	___	___	___	___
____	____	____	___	___	___	___
____	____	____	___	___	___	___

CONTINUE THIS PAGE AS NECESSARY

*OT = occupational therapy; PT = physical therapy; ST = speech therapy.

Figure 4.9 (Continued)

PART E

SUMMARIZING OFF-SITE MONITORING SERVICE SCHEDULES

Instructions. List below the number of infants and toddlers receiving off-site monitoring services and the number of hours of service received by various groups of children. Do *not* differentiate between schedules of off-site monitoring services that may have been affected by children's short-term illness or absence.

CHILDREN	SCHEDULES			TOTAL SERVICES
Column A	**Column B**	**Column C**		**Multiply Column A × B × C**
No. 99-457 Eligible Children	No. Minutes/ Visit	No. Visits/ Month	Agency Where Visit Occurred	No. Minutes/ Service/Month
___	___	___	_____	___
___	___	___	_____	___
___	___	___	_____	___
___	___	___	_____	___
___	___	___	_____	___
___	___	___	_____	___
___	___	___	_____	___
___	___	___	_____	___
___	___	___	_____	___
___	___	___	_____	___

CONTINUE THIS PAGE AS NECESSARY

Figure 4.9 (Continued)

PART F
DOCUMENTING CHILD-FIND ACTIVITIES

Instructions. Describe below the number of child-find activities that have been conducted during the reporting period, the type of activity, and the approximate number of families exposed to the activity (if this can be determined). Examples of such activities include prescreening clinics in shopping centers, reviews of high-risk registries, visits to PTA groups, and so forth.

Child Find Activity	Number of Occurrences	Approximate Number Families Exposed
_____	_____	_____
_____	_____	_____
_____	_____	_____
_____	_____	_____
_____	_____	_____
_____	_____	_____
_____	_____	_____
_____	_____	_____
_____	_____	_____
_____	_____	_____

CONTINUE THIS PAGE AS NECESSARY

Figure 4.9 (Continued)

PART G
SUMMARIZING SCREENING AND DIAGNOSTIC SERVICES TO INFANTS AND TODDLERS AND FAMILIES

Instructions. List below the number of screening and diagnostic assessments that have been conducted by your program (or your contracting program) for infants and toddlers and their families prior to or after their admittance to your program. Specify the type of screenings or assessments that were conducted as well as the number of such screenings or assessments conducted during the quarter.

Indicate Number

Prior to Enrollment	Following Enrollment	Type of Screening or Assessment
		INFANT/TODDLER
___	___	Speech/Language
___	___	Physical
___	___	Cognitive
___	___	Self-help
___	___	Psychosocial
___	___	Audiological
___	___	Vision
___	___	Medical
___	___	Health
___	___	Nutrition
___	___	Psycho-educational
___	___	Other: _____

Indicate Number

Prior to Enrollment	Following Enrollment	Type of Screening or Assessment
		FAMILY SCREENING/ASSESSMENT
___	___	Specify type: _____
___	___	Specify type: _____
___	___	Specify type: _____
___	___	Specify type: _____
___	___	Specify type: _____
___	___	Specify type: _____

CONTINUE THIS PAGE AS NECESSARY

Figure 4.9 (Continued)

PART H

DOCUMENTING EXTERNAL REFERRAL ACTIVITIES FOR INFANTS AND TODDLERS AND FAMILIES

Instructions. List below the number of infants and toddlers and their families who were referred to other agencies during the reporting period and the agencies to which the referrals were made.

Number of Children	Agency to Which Referral Was Made
_____	_____
_____	_____
_____	_____
_____	_____
_____	_____
_____	_____
_____	_____
_____	_____
_____	_____
_____	_____
_____	_____

CONTINUE THIS PAGE AS NECESSARY

Figure 4.9 (Continued)

PART I
DOCUMENTING FAMILY TRAINING AND COUNSELING SERVICES

Instructions. List below the number of families who received parent training or parent counseling during the reporting period. Also, indicate the duration of that training as well as the content of that training. Recall that this category is to be used only for families of children enrolled in the program. Recall also that this category is to be used only for "formal" training or counseling efforts (i.e., not occurring during a casual conversation between a staff member and a parent).

Number of Parents	Number of Hours	Description of Content

CONTINUE THIS PAGE AS NECESSARY

Figure 4.9 (Continued)

PART J
DESCRIBING TRAINING AND TECHNICAL ASSISTANCE TO OTHER PROVIDERS

Instructions. List below the number of other early intervention providers whom you have trained or who have received technical assistance from your program or contracted program. Specify also the time spent on that training or technical assistance as well as the content of that training.

Number of Recipients	Number of Hours	Type of Persons	Description of Content

CONTINUE THIS PAGE AS NECESSARY

Figure 4.9 (Continued)

PART K

DESCRIBING WAITING LISTS AND WAITING LIST ACTIVITY

Instructions. List below the number of infants and toddlers who are on waiting lists for your program as well as the reasons why those children are not being served. Additionally, list the number of children who may be receiving some form of intervention services and describe those services (typically monitoring or brief home visits).

Number of 99-457 Eligible Children on Waiting List	Length of Time on Waiting List	Reason for Placement on Waiting List
_____	_____	_____
_____	_____	_____
	_____	_____

Number of 99-457 Eligible Waiting List Children Receiving Services		Type of Services
_____	_____	_____
_____	_____	_____
_____	_____	_____
_____	_____	_____

CONTINUE THIS PAGE AS NECESSARY

Figure 4.9 (Continued)

PART L

DESCRIBING FUNDING SOURCES OF EARLY INTERVENTION

Instructions. Describe below the funds expended specifically for early intervention services to P.L. 99-457 eligible infants and toddlers and their families (include cost of screening to determine eligibility). Do not include costs associated with capital outlays (building and construction). Provide the amount of funds expended during the reporting cycle by each source category (i.e., federal, state, and local sources). If possible, each entry should represent actual expenditures. Indicate if the expenditures provided represent actual expenditures or estimated expenditures by placing an X in the appropriate blank.

Source	Funds	Estimated? (Indicate X)
Federal	____	____
State	____	____
Local	____	____

Figure 4.9 (Continued)

PART M
DESCRIBING EARLY INTERVENTION NEEDS

Instructions. Indicate in narrative form early intervention services in need of improvement in the geographic area served by your program. Improved services consist of services that are (a) not currently available for handicapped infants and toddlers; (b) in short supply for specific populations; and (c) in a stage where considerable development is necessary for the service to have maximum effectiveness or be delivered efficiently.

Indicate three to five early intervention services in greatest need of improvement and rank those services (if possible) according to need (i.e., #1 is the highest priority need, #2 is the second highest priority need, etc.).

For each service needing improvement, provide a brief narrative description of the nature of improvement(s) needed. In this narrative, include the number of handicapped infants and toddlers in need of improved services and the number and type of personnel needed to provide these services.

_____

_____

_____

_____

_____

_____

_____

_____

management programs to create computerized screens looking very similar to the actual data collection sheets. These programs also check for inconsistency of reported data and generate reports for any desired reporting cycle.

Data gathered from the Early Intervention Services Report (Figure 4.9) can be used to report to the federal government, Office of Special Education programs on tables 1, 2, 4, and 5 of OSEP Memorandum (1988). To date, this request for information is all that is being made of state-designated lead agencies by the federal government. We do anticipate additional requests being made of states, although we are confident that the instruments presented in this text will be sufficient to address data collection requests for the foreseeable future.

Epilogue

The ending of this book represents a true beginning for infants and toddlers and their families in this country. Tjossem's (1976) statement cited in Chapter 1 is worth repeating.

> Prevention of mental retardation and related developmental disabilities is the ultimate goal of our national effort to combat these disorders. (p. 3)

The passage of P.L. 99-457, and its implementation during the next several years, represents a significant step in our nation's commitment to the disabled children in this country and their families.

We are well aware of the difficulties facing early intervention providers in designing and implementing comprehensive early intervention systems. Existing early intervention systems must be modified, and new systems must be created. Long-standing practices must be re-examined and ways must be found to chart a clear path for every child and family through the maze of bureaucracies that will contribute to the unified, comprehensive system.

The congressional authors of P.L. 99-457, the Ninty-ninth Congress of the United States, and the president of the United States have made it clear that handicapped infants and toddlers should be served from the moment their disability is detected. They have also opened the door for states to help reduce the incidence of disability by permitting states to include at-risk children and families in their comprehensive statewide early intervention systems. The birth of a handicapped child, or the detection of a child with a disability, should signal the initiation of a well-developed, interagency system. This system should put in place a competent, caring case manager who will advocate for children and their families throughout the early childhood years to ensure delivery of appropriate early intervention services.

This book represents an attempt to provide guidance to early intervention specialists who are working at the forefront of the early intervention effort. In several years we would like to see another book that represents "best practices" in designing and implementing statewide comprehensive early intervention systems. The passage of P.L. 99-457 represents an honest, hopeful beginning in this nation's efforts to help every child and family lead happy, productive lives.

References

Abeson, A., & Zettel, J. (1977). The end of the quiet revolution: The Education for All Handicapped Children Act of 1975. *Exceptional Children, 44,* 114–130.

Alpern, G., & Shearer, M. (1980). *Developmental profile.* Aspen, CO: Psychological Development Publications.

Andrews, S. R., Blumenthal, J. B., Johnson, D. L., Kahn, A. J., Ferguson, C. J., Lasater, T. M., Malone, P. E., & Wallace, D. B. (1982). The skills of mothering: A study of parent child development centers. *Monographs of the Society for Research in Child Development, 47*(6, Serial No. 198).

Austin, C. (1983). Case management in long-term care: Options and opportunities. *Health and Social Work, 8*(1), 16–30.

Bayley, N. (1969). *Bayley Scales of Infant Development.* New York: Psychological Corp.

Bloom, B. J. (1964). *Stability and change in human characteristics.* New York: Wiley.

Bourland, B., & Harbin, G. (1987). *START resource packet: CHILD FIND.* Chapel Hill: Frank Porter Graham Child Development Center–University of North Carolina at Chapel Hill.

Bricker, D. D. (Ed.). (1982). *Intervention with at-risk and handicapped infants.* Austin, TX: PRO-ED.

Bricker, D., Squires, J., Kaminski, R., & Monents, L. (in press). *Journal of Pediatric Psychology.*

Bristol, M. (1987). Methodological caveats in the assessment of single-parent families of handicapped children. *Journal of the Division for Early Childhood, 11*(2), 135–142.

Bronfenbrenner, U. (1969). Motivational and social components in compensatory education programs: Suggested principles, practices, and research designs. In E. Grotberg (Ed.), *Critical issues in research relating to disadvantaged children.* Princeton, NJ: Educational Testing Service.

Burke, P. J., McLaughlin, M. J., & Valdivieso, C. H. (1988). Preparing professionals to educate handicapped infants and young children: Some policy considerations. *Topics in Early Childhood Special Education, 8*(1), 73–80.

Campbell, P. H., Bellamy, G. T., & Bishop, K. K. (1988). Statewide intervention systems: An overview of the new federal program for infants and toddlers with handicaps. *The Journal of Special Education, 22,* 25–40.

Casto, G., & Mastropieri, M. (1986). The efficacy of early intervention programs: A meta-analysis. *Exceptional Children, 52,* 417–424.

Dunst, C. J., & Trivette, C. M. (in press). An enablement and empowerment perspective of case management. *Topics in Early Childhood Special Education, 8*(4).

Education of the Handicapped Act. 20 U.S.C. 1401.

Elder, J. O. (1980). Writing interagency agreements. In J. O. Elder & P. R. Magrab (Eds.), *Coordinating services to handicapped children: A handbook for interagency collaboration.* Baltimore: Paul H. Brookes.

Fewell, R. R. (1983). Assessing handicapped infants. In S. G. Garwood & R. R. Fewell (Eds.), *Educating handicapped infants: Issues in development and intervention.* Rockville, MD: Aspen Systems.

Fraas, C. J. (1986). *Preschool programs for the education of handicapped children: Background, issues, and federal policy options* (Congressional Research Service, Report No. 86–55 EPW). Washington, DC: Library of Congress.

Garland, C., Woodruff, G., & Buck, D. M. (1988, June). *Case management.* Division for Early Childhood White Paper, The Council for Exceptional Children.

Garwood, S. G. (1981). Assessment: The need for positive skepticism. *Topics in Early Childhood Special Education, 1*(2), viii–ix.

Garwood, S. G. (Ed.). (1983a). *Educating young handicapped children: A developmental approach* (2nd ed.). Rockville, MD: Aspen Systems.

Garwood, S. G. (1983b). The role of theory in studying infant behavior. In S. G. Garwood & R. R. Fewell (Eds.), *Educating handicapped infants: Issues in development and intervention.* Rockville, MD: Aspen Systems.

Garwood, S. G., Fewell, R. R., & Neisworth, J. T. (1988). Public Law 94-142: You can get there from here! *Topics in Early Childhood Special Education, 8*(1), 1–11.

Garwood, S. G., Phillips, D., Hartman, A., & Zigler, E. (1989). As the pendulum swings: Federal agency programs for children. *American Psychologist, 44,* 434–440.

Gradel, K. (1988). Interface between assessment and intervention for infants and preschoolers with disabilities. In T. D. Wachs & R. Sheehan (Eds.), *Assessment of young developmentally disabled children* (pp. 373–395). New York: Plenum.

Guralnick, M. J., & Bennett, F. C. (Eds.). (1987). *The effectiveness of early intervention for at-risk and handicapped children.* New York: Academic Press.

Hanson, M. J. (Ed.). (1984). *Atypical infant development.* Austin, TX: PRO-ED.

Harbin, G. L. (1988). Implementatin of P.L. 99-457: State technical assistance. *Topics in Early Childhood Special Education, 8*(1), 24–36.

Hess, R. D., & Shipman, V. C. (1965). Early experience and the socialization of cognitive modes in children. *Child Development, 36,* 869–886.

House Report 99-860. (1986). U.S. House of Representatives. Washington, DC: Government Printing Office.

Hunt, J. McV. (1961). *Intelligence and experience.* New York: Ronald Press.

Intagliata, J. (1982). Improving the quality of community care for the chronically mentally disabled: The role of case management. *Schizophrenia Bulletin, 8*(1), 655–673.

Leventhal, J. M., & Sabbeth, B. A. (1986). The family and chronic illness in children. In M. W. Yogman & T. B. Brazelton (Eds.), *In support of families*. Cambridge, MA: Harvard University Press.

Lewis, J. M., Beavers, W. R., Gossett, J. T., & Phillips, V. A. (1976). *No single thread: Psychological health in family systems*. New York: Bruner/Mazel.

Meisels, S. J. (1985). The efficacy of early intervention: Why are we still asking this question? *Topics in Early Childhood Special Education, 5*(2), 1–11.

Meisels, S. J., Harbin, G. L., Modigliani, K., & Olsen, K. (1988). Formulating optimal state early childhood intervention policies. *Exceptional Children, 55*(2), 159–165.

Miller, G. E. (1983). Case management: The essential service. In C. J. Sanborn (Ed.), *Case management in mental health services*. New York: Haworth.

Miller, G. E. (1984). The future of the chronically mentally ill. In M. Mirabi & L. Feldman (Eds.), *The chronically mentally ill: Research and services*. New York: SP Medical & Scientific Books.

Minahan, A. (Ed.). (1987). *Encyclopedia of social work* (18th ed.). Silver Spring, MD: National Association of Social Workers.

NCCIP. (1986). *Infants can't wait: The numbers*. Washington, DC: The National Clinical Center for Infant Programs.

Odom, S. L., Yoder, P., & Hill, G. (1988). Developmental intervention for infants with handicaps: Purposes and programs. *The Journal of Special Education, 22*, 11–24.

Parent Resource Directory (2nd ed.). (1988). Washington, DC: Association for the Care of Children's Health.

Robinson, C., & Fieber, N. (1988). Cognitive assessment of motorically impaired infants and preschoolers. In T. D. Wachs & R. Sheehan (Eds.), *Assessment of young developmentally disabled children* (pp. 127–162). New York: Plenum.

Sheehan, R., & Sites, J. (in press). Implications of P.L. 99-457 for assessment. *Topics in Early Childhood Special Education*.

Shonkoff, J. P., Hauser-Cram, P., Krauss, M. W., & Upshur, C. C. (1988). Early intervention efficacy research: What have we learned and where do we go from here? *Topics in Early Childhood Special Education, 8*(1), 81–93.

Smith, B. J., & Strain, P. S. (1988). Early childhood special education in the next decade: Implementing and expanding P.L. 99-457. *Topics in Early Childhood Special Education, 8*(1), 37–46.

Steiner, G. Y. (1976). *The children's cause*. Washington, DC: The Brookings Institution.

Stinnett, N., Chesser, B., & DeFrain, J. (1979). *Building family strengths: Blueprints for action*. Lincoln: University of Nebraska Press.

Tjossem, T. D. (Ed.). (1976). *Intervention strategies for high risk infants and young children*. Baltimore: University Park Press.

Trohanis, P., & Decker, M. (1987). *START resource packet: PUBLIC AWARENESS*. Chapel Hill: Frank Porter Graham Child Development Center–University of North Carolina at Chapel Hill.

USDOE. (1985). *Seventh annual report to Congress on the implementation of the Education of the Handicapped Act*. Washington, DC: Government Printing Office.

USDOE. (1987). *Ninth annual report to Congress on the implementation of the Education of the Handicapped Act*. Washington, DC: Government Printing Office.

Wachs, T. D., & Sheehan, R. (1988b). Issues in the linkage of assessment to intervention. In T. Wachs & R. Sheehan (Eds.), *Assessment of young developmentally disabled children* (pp. 397–406). New York: Plenum.

Wachs, T. D., & Sheehan, R. (Eds.). (1988a). *Assessment of young developmentally disabled children.* New York: Plenum.

White, K., & Casto, G. (1985). An integrative review of early intervention efficacy studies with at-risk children: Implications for the handicapped. *Analysis and Intervention in Developmental Disabilities, 5,* 177–201.

Winton, P., & Turnbull, A. (1981). Parent involvement as viewed by parents of preschool handicapped children. *Topics in Early Childhood Special Education, 1*(3), 11–20.

Appendix 1

State Agencies and Contact Persons

Alabama
Patricia A. Patton, Supervisor
Crippled Children Services
State Department of Education
2129 East South Boulevard
Montgomery, AL 36199-3801
(205) 288-0220

Alaska
Karen Lamb, ILP Education
   Specialist
State Department of Health and
   Social Services
1231 Gambell Street
Anchorage, AK 99501
(907) 278-3841

American Samoa
Julia Lyons, Project Coordinator
LBJ Tropical Medical Center
Department of Health
Government of American Samoa
Pago Pago, AS 96799
011 (684) 633-4929

Arizona
David Oake, Program Services
   Manager
Division of Developmental Disabilities
Department of Economic Security
1400 West Washington Street

P.O. Box 6760
Phoenix, AZ 85005
(602) 255-5775

Arkansas
Kellie Jennings, Early Intervention
   Coordinator
Division of Developmental Disabilities
   Services
Department of Human Services
P.O. Box 1437
Waldon Building, 5th Floor
7th and Main Streets
Little Rock, AR 72203-1437
(501) 682-8662

Bureau of Indian Affairs
Charles Cordova, Chief
Branch of Exceptional Education
Office of Indian Education Programs
Bureau of Indian Affairs
MS 4659 (MIB)
18th and C Streets, N.W.
Washington, DC 20245
(202) 343-1990 or 343-4071

California
Paul D. Carleton
Deputy Director
Community Services Division

169

Department of Developmental
Services
P.O. Box 944202
Sacramento, CA 94244-2020
(916) 323-4828

Colorado
Elizabeth Soper, Coordinator
Diane Garner, Consultant
Special Education Division
State Department of Education
201 East Colfax, Room 301
Denver, CO 80203
(303) 866-6710

Connecticut
Virginia Volk, Coordinator
Early Childhood Unit
State Department of Education
P.O. Box 2219
Hartford, CT 06145
(203) 566-6584

Delaware
Deborah A. Ziegler, Director
Delaware Early Childhood Diagnostic
and Intervention Center
Lake Forest South B Elementary
Mispillian and West Streets
Harrington, DE 19952
(302) 398-8945 or 736-4557

**Department of Defense
Dependent Schools**
Trudy Paul
Department of Defense Dependent
Schools
Hoffman Building #2
2461 Eisenhower Avenue
Alexandria, VA 22331-1100
(703) 325-7810

District of Columbia
Barbara Ferguson Kamara
Executive Director
Office of Early Childhood
Development
Commission on Social Services
Randall Building, Suite 224

First and "I" Streets, S.W.
Washington, DC 20024
(202) 727-5947

**Federated States of Micronesia
(FSM)**
Yosiro Suta
(619) Coordinator
Federal Education Program
Federated States of Micronesia
Office of Education
Kolonia, Panape
East Caroline Islands 96941
01-691-9-609
Note: No contact person for Part H
available

Florida
Nancy Thomas, Administrator
Office of Early Intervention
State Department of Education
Knott Building
Tallahassee, FL 32399
(904) 488-6830

Dr. William Ausbon, Director
Children's Medical Services
Department of Health and
Rehabilitative Services
1317 Winewood Boulevard
Tallahassee, FL 32399
(904) 488-3905

Georgia
Ralph McCuin, Director
Heather McCabe, Coordinator
Mental Retardation Section
Developmental Services Unit
Department of Human Resources
878 Peachtree Street, Suite 310
Atlanta, GA 30309-3999
(404) 894-6329 (McCuin)
894-6331 (McCabe)

Guam
Steve Spencer
Assoc. Superintendent for Special
Education
Special Education Division
Department of Education

P.O. Box DE
Agana, GU 96910
011 (671) 472-8901

Hawaii
Darryl Leong, Chief
Crippled Children Services Branch
Family Health Services Division
Department of Health
741 Sunset Avenue
Honolulu, HI 98616
(808) 732-3197

Jean L. Stewart, Coordinator
Zero-to-Three Hawaii Project
Diamond Head Health Center,
  Rm. 106
3627 Kilauea Avenue
Honolulu, HI 96816
(808) 735-0434

Idaho
Paul Swatsenbarg, Chief
Katherine Pavesic, Project Mananger
  for Part H
Bureau of Developmental Disabilities
Department of Health and Welfare
450 West State Street, 10th Floor
Boise, ID 83720
(208) 334-5531

Illinois
Jonah Deppe, Early Childhood
  Specialist
Department of Special Education
State Board of Education
100 North First Street
Springfield, IL 62777
(217) 782-6601

Indiana
Doree Bedwell, Director
Early Intervention Project
Sheron Cochran, Quality Assurance
  Coordinator
Division of Developmental Disabilities
Department of Mental Health
117 East Washington Street
Indianapolis, IN 46204
(317) 232-7836

Iowa
Peggy Cvach, ESCE Consultant
Bureau of Special Education
Department of Public Instruction
Grimes State Office Building
Des Moines, IA 50319-0146
(515) 281-3176

Kansas
July Moler, Executive Coordinator
Coordinating Council on Early
  Childhood Developmental Services
Dr. Virginia Tucker, Director
Maternal and Child Health
State Department of Health and
  Environment
Landon State Office Building
900 S.W. Jackson, 10th Floor
Topeka, KS 66620-0001
(913) 296-1329 (Moler)
      296-1305 (Tucker)

Kentucky
Marge Allen
Department of Mental Health and
  Mental Retardation
275 East Main Street
Frankfort, KY 40621
(502) 564-7700

Louisiana
Ronald LaCoste, Bureau Director
Evelyn Johnson, Interagency
  Coordinator
Office of Special Educational Services
State Department of Education
P.O. Box 94064
Baton Rouge, LA 70804-9064
(504) 342-3631

Maine
Susan Mackey-Andrews
Early Childhood Services
Division of Special Education
Department of Education and
  Cultural Services
State House, Station #23
Augusta, ME 04333
(207) 289-5950

Republic of the Marshall Islands (RMI)
Teruo Kaminaga, Assistant Director
 for Special Education
Karen Dribo, Spec. Ed.
 Director's Representative
Department of Education
P.O. Box 3
Republic of the Marshall Islands
Majuro, Marshall Islands 96960

Maryland
Dianne Madoni, Acting Director
Governor's Office for Children and
 Youth
Carol Baglin, Project Director
Infants & Toddlers Program
1123 N. Eutaw Street, Room 601
Baltimore, MD 21201
(301) 333-5800 (Madoni)
        333-5720 (Baglin)

Massachusetts
Karl Kastorf, Director
Early Childhood Developmental
 Services Unit
Division of Family Health Services
Department of Public Health
150 Tremont Street
Boston, MA 02111
(617) 727-5090

Michigan
Carolyn Logan, Supervisor
Early Childhood Education
State Department of Education
P.O. Box 30008
Lansing, MI 48909
(517) 373-8483

Minnesota
Jan Rubenstein, Coordinator
Interagency Planning Project for
 Young Children with Handicaps
Capitol Square Building, 8th Floor
550 Cedar Street
St. Paul, MN 55101
(612) 296-7032

Martha Smith, Planner
IPPYCH
State Department of Health
P.O. Box 9441
717 Delaware Street, S.E.
Minneapolis, MN 55440
(612) 623-5538

Mississippi
Sam Valentine, Director
Children's Medical Program
Norciva Geddie, Branch Director II
State Board of Health
P.O. Box 1700
2423 North State Street
Jackson, MS 39215-1700
(601) 960-7613

Missouri
John Heskett, Coordinator
Section of Special Education
Department of Elementary and
 Secondary Education
P.O. Box 480
Jefferson City, MO 65102
(314) 751-2965

Montana
Mike Hanshew, Chief
Management Operations Bureau
Richard Van Haeke, Early
 Intervention Specialist
Developmental Disabilities Division
Department of Social and
 Rehabilitation Services
P.O. Box 4210
Helena, MT 59604
(406) 444-2995

Nebraska
Gary M. Sherman, Director
Karen Stevens, Consultant
Special Education Section
State Department of Education
P.O. Box 94987
Lincoln, NE 68509
(402) 471-2471

Nevada
Marilyn Walter
Department of Human Resources
Office of the Director
505 East King Street
Carson City, NV 89710
(702) 885-4730

New Hampshire
Luzanne Pierce
Office of Special Education
State Department of Education
State Office Park, South
101 Pleasant Street
Concord, NH 03301
(603) 271-3493

New Jersey
Noreen Gallagher, Manager
Arlene Roth, Assistant Manager
Early Childhood Education
Division of Special Education
State Department of Education
225 West State Street, CN 500
Trenton, NJ 08625
(609) 633-6951

New Mexico
Louis Worley
Developmental Disabilities Bureau
Department of Health and
  Environment
P.O. Box 968
Santa Fe, NM 87504-0968
(505) 827-0118

New York
Frank Zollo
Bureau of Child and Adolescent
  Health
Department of Health
Corning Tower, Room 780
Empire State Plaza
Albany, NY 12237
(518) 474-2093

North Carolina
Duncan E. Munn
Chief of Day Services

Mental Health, Mental Retardation,
  and Substance Abuse Services
Department of Human Resources
325 North Salisbury Street
Raleigh, NC 27611
(919) 733-3654

North Dakota
Shelby Niebergall
Developmental Disabilities Division
Department of Human Services
State Capitol
Bismarck, ND 58505
(701) 224-2768

Northern Mariana Islands
Josephine Sablan, Assistant
  Coordinator
Early Childhood Special Education
  Program
Department of Education
Commonwealth of the Northern
  Mariana Islands
Lower Base
Saipan, CM 96950
011 (670) 322-9956 or 322-9256

Ohio
James Quilty, Chief
Kathryn Peppe, Nursing Consultant
Division of Maternal and Child
  Health
State Department of Health
P.O. Box 118
Columbus, OH 43266-0118
(614) 466-3263 (Quilty)
      466-4644 (Peppe)

Oklahoma
Earlene Belling
Early Intervention Coordinator
Special Education Office
State Department of Education
Oliver Hodge Memorial Education
  Building, Suite 269
2500 North Lincoln Boulevard
Oklahoma City, OK 73105
(405) 751-0065

Oregon
Mike Baker, Coordinator
Early Intervention
Mental Health Division
Department of Human Resources
2575 Bittern Street, N.E.
Salem, OR 97310
(503) 378-2004 or 378-4765

Republic of Palau
Peter Elechuus, Coordinator
Special Education
Masa-Aki Emesiochel, Chief
Division of Curriculum Development
Bureau of Education
P.O. Box 189
Koror, Palau 96940
01-952-568 (Elechuus)
01-570 or 479 (Emesiochel)

Pennsylvania
Mel Knowlton, Director
Bureau of Program Development and
   Policy
Office of Mental Retardation
Health and Welfare Building,
   Room 302
Harrisburg, PA 17120
(717) 783-5758

Puerto Rico
Awilda Torres
Director for Early Childhood
Carmen Aviles, Special Education
   Supervisor
Infant and Toddlers Program
Department of Education
P.O. Box 759
Hato Rey, PR 00919
(809) 754-0094 (Torres)
      751-5372 (Aviles)

Rhode Island
Thomas Kochanek
Executive Director
Interagency Coordinating Council
Department of Special Education
Rhode Island College

600 Mt. Pleasant Avenue
Providence, RI, 02908
(401) 456-8599

South Carolina
Ann Wall Lee, Director
Division of Children's Health
Department of Health and
   Environmental Control
2600 Bull Street
Columbia, SC 29201
(803) 734-4610

South Dakota
Paulette Levisen
Section for Special Education
Department of Education and
   Cultural Affairs
700 Governors Drive
Pierre, SD 57501-3133
(605) 773-4693

Tennessee
Joleta Reynolds, Associate Assistant
   Commissioner
Office for Special Education
State Department of Education
100 Cordell Hull Building
Nashville, TN 37219
(615) 741-2851

Texas
Mary Jo Miller, TA Coordinator
Early Childhood Intervention Program
State Department of Mental
   Health/Mental Retardation
P.O. Box 12668
Austin, Texas 78711
(512) 465-4668

Jill Gray, Director
Special Education Program
Texas Education Agency
1701 North Congress
Austin, Texas 78701
(512) 463-9414

Utah
Dr. George Delavan, Director
Chris Kaminsky, Coordinator
Early Intervention Program
Handicapped Children's Services
State Department of Health
P.O. Box 11650-15HCS (Delavan)
P.O. Box 11650-25HCS (Kaminsky)
Salt Lake City, UT 84116-0650
(801) 538-6165 (Delavan)
      538-6922 (Kaminsky)

Vermont
Kristin Reedy
Special Education Unit
State Department of Education
120 State Street
Montpelier, VT 05602-2703
(803) 828-3141

Virgin Islands
Patricia Adams, Program Director
Iselyne Hennessey, Project Director
Division of Maternal and Child
   Health/Crippled Children Services
Department of Health
Knud Hansen Complex
St. Thomas, VI 00802
(809) 776-3580 (Adams)
      774-9000 (Hennessey)

Virginia
Michael Fehl, Director
Mental Retardation, Children and
   Youth Services
Cynthia Jones, Coordinator
Early Intervention Program
Department of Mental Health, Mental
   Retardation and Substance Abuse
   Services

P.O. Box 1797
Richard VA 23233
(804) 786-3710

Washington
Susan Baxter, Interagency
   Coordinator
OSPI/DCFS Project C
Department of Social and Health
   Services
12th and Franklin Streets
Olympia, WA 98504-4151
(206) 753-1233

West Virginia
Wanda Radcliff, Specialist
Early Intervention and Family
   Support
State Department of Health
1800 Washington Street, East
Capitol Complex, Room 458
Charleston, WV 25305
(304) 348-2276

Wisconsin
Gareth Johnson, Director
Maternal and Child Health Programs
Wisconsin Division of Health
P.O. Box 7850
Madison, WI 53707
(608) 266-2670

Wyoming
Ken B. Heinlein, Program Manager
Division of Community Programs
Department of Health and Social
   Services
354 Hathaway Building
Cheyenne, WY 82002
(307) 777-7115

Appendix 2

United States Department of Education Memorandum (OSEP-88-12)

MEMORANDUM

UNITED STATES DEPARTMENT OF EDUCATION
WASHINGTON, D.C. 20202

DATE: February 10, 1988

| Contact Person |
| Name: Kathleen Hebbeler |
| Telephone: (202) 732-1010 |

OSEP MEMORANDUM

| OSEP-88-12 |

To: Contact Person, Part H Lead Agency

From: G. Thomas Bellamy, Ph.D., Director
Office of Special Education Programs

Subject: Data Collection for Part H of the Education
of the Handicapped Act

Attached are the instructions and data collection forms you are
to use for reporting data related to Part H of the Education of
the Handicapped Act. Please note that only data for number of
children served are requested for 1987-88 and submission of
these data is not a program requirement. If the Table 1 data
are available to you or can be collected with reasonable effort,
please provide them. States who are unable to provide any data
should notify us to that effect. We encourage you to call Kathy
Hebbeler if you have any questions about the data requested
or if you need any additional information about how to collect
them.

We are providing the forms at this time to inform you of the
data that will be required in the future. This information
should help you in developing your data collection system. We
understand that a number of States currently have no system
in place to collect the kind of information requested. On the
other hand, there is and will continue to be much Congres-

Page 2—Memo to Part H Contact Person

sional interest in the number of infants and toddlers being assisted through Part H. If you already have or will soon be developing the capability to collect these and the other data requested, we would like to be able to report the information as soon as possible.

We are planning to provide various kinds of assistance to States in the development of a data system over the next several years. The exact mechanisms for this assistance have not yet been worked out, but we will keep you informed. Mechanisms currently available to you include the Early Childhood Technical Assistance Center (EC/TAC) at the University of North Carolina and the Regional Resource Center for your area. EC/TAC will be contacting you shortly if they haven't already.

If you are in a State where Special Education is not the lead agency, you may not be aware that data on various features of special education for older children are submitted annually by your State. The forms used are similar to the Part H forms. Your State may be able to adapt the system it is currently using for the school-aged data to meet the Part H requirements.

OSEP is proposing the following submission schedule for the enclosed data tables.

Form	Based on Data Collected on:	Due to OSEP on:	Status:
1987-88 School Year:			
Table 1	Dec. 1, 1987	April 4, 1988	Voluntary
Table 2-5		Not Requested	
1988-89 School Year:			
Table 1	Dec. 1, 1988	Feb. 1, 1989	Required
Table 2-3	Dec. 1, 1988	Nov. 1, 1989	Voluntary
Table 4		Not Requested	
Table 5	Not Applicable	Nov. 1, 1989	Voluntary

Page 3—Memo to Part H Contact Person

Form	Based on Data Collected on:	Due to OSEP on:	Status:

1989-90 School Year (and thereafter):

Table 1	Dec. 1, 1989	Feb. 1, 1990	Required
Table 2-3	Dec. 1, 1989	Nov. 1, 1990	Required
Table 4	1987-88 Sch. Yr.	Nov. 1, 1990	Required
Table 5	Not Applicable	Nov. 1, 1990	Required

Before officially adopting the schedule of due dates above, OSEP is interested in hearing from States regarding State capacity to meet these timelines. Please forward comments to Kathy Hebbeler.

Send Table 1 data (or your reason for not submitting them) by April 4, 1988, to:

> Kathy Hebbeler
> Switzer Building: Mail Stop 2313/3094
> Office of Special Education Programs
> 400 Maryland Avenue, S.W.
> Washington, DC 20202

TABLE 1

REPORT OF HANDICAPPED INFANTS AND TODDLERS RECEIVING EARLY INTERVENTION SERVICES UNDER PART B AND PART H OF THE EDUCATION OF THE HANDICAPPED ACT, AS AMENDED

This report is authorized under 20 U.S.C. 1476(b)(14) and 1418(b)(1).

Instructions

General Instructions

1. For this report, do not include infants and toddlers counted by a State agency under Section 146 of Title I as incorporated by Section 554 of the Education Consolidation and Improvement Act of 1981 (Chapter 1, State Operated Programs for Handicapped Children).

2. Count and report all handicapped infants and toddlers receiving early intervention services according to an individualized family service plan. This must be an unduplicated count (i.e., each handicapped infant and toddler is represented only once on this data table).

3. To the extent possible, we are interested in counts as of December 1, 1987. (December 1 will be the count for all future years.) If numbers for that date are not available, report data for the closest possible date.

4. Forms are to be submitted to the Department of Education, Office of Special Education Programs (OSEP), Division of Innovation and Development by April 4, 1988.

Specific Instructions

Section B

Enter the total number of handicapped infants and toddlers birth through age 2 receiving early intervention services on December 1, 1987 (or as close to that date as possible). Children should be reported based on their age on December 1.

Include in these counts individuals from birth through age 2 (children who have not yet reached their third birthday) who are experiencing developmental delays or have a diagnosed physical or mental condition which has a high probability of resulting in developmental delay. If your State has elected to serve children who are at risk of having substantial delays if early intervention services are not provided, include these children in the count. Children counted are those who are receiving developmental services which—

    a. are provided under public supervision;

    b. are provided at no cost except where Federal or State law provides for a system of payments, including a schedule of sliding fees;

Page 2

   c. are designed to meet a handicapped infant's or toddler's developmental needs; and

   d. are provided in conformity with an individualized family service plan.

Data for each discrete age and for the age grouping 0 through 2 are required. Children less than one year of age should be counted in the "0 to 1" cell. States that have discrete age data available should base the report on these actual data. States that do not have data for each discrete age are required to report actual data for the age grouping 0 through 2 and to estimate data for discrete ages.

Section C

Enter the total number of infants and toddlers aged 0 through 2 who have been evaluated and determined to be in need of early intervention services and who were *not* receiving these services on December 1, 1987 (or as close to that date as possible). This count may be based on a sampling of data from State agencies including State and local service agencies. When sampling is used, a description of the sampling methodology must be submitted to OSEP for approval.

TABLE 2

REPORT OF EARLY INTERVENTION SERVICES PROVIDED TO HANDICAPPED INFANTS, TODDLERS, AND THEIR FAMILIES

1988–1989 SCHOOL YEAR

Instructions

This report is authorized under 20 U.S.C. 1476(b)(14) and 1418(b)(i).

General Instructions

Enter a duplicated count of handicapped infants and toddlers according to the early intervention services that they receive. Early intervention services are developmental services which (a) are provided under public supervision; (b) are provided at no cost except where Federal or State law provides for a system of payments, including a schedule of sliding fees; (c) are designed to meet a handicapped infant's or toddler's developmental needs; and (d) are provided in conformity with an individualized family service plan.

Infants, toddlers, and their families receiving more than one type of early intervention service should be counted under each service they are receiving. Do not report duplicated counts within service categories. Data reported for this table are to be based on the Child and Youth Counts of October 1, Chapter 1, ECIA (SOP) and December 1, EHA-B/H. Where data cells contain no numeric value, please place zeroes (0). If any of the service categories are not used in the State, please indicate by coding (-9).

Forms are due by November 1, 1989.

Specific Instructions

Row 1   Psychological Services include:

- Obtaining, integrating, and interpreting information about child behavior and conditions relating to learning;

- Consulting with other staff members in planning programs to meet the special needs of children as indicated by psychological tests, interviews, and behavioral evaluations;

- Planning and managing a program of psychological services, including psychological counseling for families; and

- Administering and interpreting psychological tests, and other assessment procedures during the reevaluation of handicapped children.

Row 2   Family Training, Counseling, and Home Visits include:

- Preparing a social or developmental history on a handicapped infant or toddler;

Page 2

- Group and individual training and counseling with families of handicapped infants and toddlers; and

- Working with those problems in an infant's or toddler's living situation that affect the child's development in one or more of the following areas: cognitive development, physical development, language and speech development, psychosocial development, or self-help skills.

- No single service is to be counted in more than one row. If a child received family training, counseling, or home visits as part of another service listed below (for example, a home visit performed by a psychologist), count the service under Row 2.

Row 3   Occupational Therapy includes:

- Developing posture and movement abilities;

- Improving, developing, or restoring functions impaired or lost through illness, injury, or deprivation; and

- Preventing, through early intervention, initial or further impairment or loss of function.

Row 4   Speech-Language Pathology includes:

- Developing and enhancing communication skills;

- Diagnosis and appraisal of developmental lags in speech and language development;

- Referral for medical or other professional attention necessary for the habilitation of speech or language disorders; and

- Counseling and guidance of families regarding speech and language disorders.

Row 5   Audiological Services include:

- Determination of the range, nature, and degree of hearing loss, including referral for medical or other professional attention for the rehabilitation of hearing;

- Provision of habilitative activities, such as language habilitation, auditory training, speech reading (lip-reading), hearing evaluation, and speech conservation; and

- Determination of the child's need for group and individual amplification, selecting and fitting an appropriate aid, and evaluating the effectiveness of amplification.

Page 3

Row 6   Special Instruction includes:

- Instruction provided to infants and toddlers and their families by special educators and other qualified personnel; and

- Instruction provided in the child's home and in early intervention centers, hospitals, and clinics or other settings as appropriate to the age and needs of the child.

Row 7   Physical Therapy includes services and treatment provided by a qualified physical therapist to develop posture and movement abilities.

Row 8   Medical Services include services only for diagnostic or evaluation purposes.

Row 9   Health Services include services necessary to enable a child to benefit from other early intervention services (e.g., catherization). Health Services under EHA-B/H do not include services which are surgical or purely medical in nature (e.g., cleft palate surgery, surgery for club foot, management of congenital heart ailments, management of cystic fibrosis, and shunting of hydrocephalus).

Row 10   Other Early Intervention Services include early intervention services which are not specified in this report.

TABLE 3

NUMBER AND TYPE OF PERSONNEL (In Full-Time Equivalency of Assignment) EMPLOYED AND ADDITIONAL PERSONNEL NEEDED TO PROVIDE EARLY INTERVENTION SERVICES FOR HANDICAPPED INFANTS AND TODDLERS IN THE 1988-1989 SCHOOL YEAR

Instructions

This report is authorized under 20 U.S.C. 1476(b)(14) and 1418(b)(5).

Provide the number of full-time equivalent personnel employed to provide early intervention services on or about December 1, 1988, and the number of additional qualified personnel needed for the 1988–89 school year. The table must include data from the SEA and all other agencies having responsibility for providing early intervention services for handicapped infants and toddlers. Forms are due by November 1, 1989.

The number of personnel should be reported in full-time equivalency of assignment (e.g., if two half-time personnel are employed, they would equal one full-time employee). Decimals may be used. Place zeroes (0) in categories where no personnel are employed. If any personnel categories are not used in the State, indicate by coding (-9).

For Column A, Early Intervention Services Personnel Employed, report the number of personnel employed to provide early intervention services for handicapped infants and toddlers.

Include in these figures personnel employed by public and private agencies which (1) provide developmental services that are designed to meet a handicapped infant's or toddler's developmental needs; (2) provide services under public supervision; (3) provide services at no cost except where Federal or State law provides for a system of payments by families including a schedule of sliding fees; and, (4) provide services in conformity with an individualized family service plan.

For Column B, Additional Early Intervention Personnel Needed, report the number of additional early intervention personnel needed to maintain the full educational opportunity goal to provide early intervention services for handicapped infants and toddlers.

Include in these figures:

(1) the number of unfilled vacancies that occurred during the 1988–89 school year (12 months); and

(2) the number of additional personnel that were needed during the 1988–89 school year (12 months) to fill positions occupied by persons who were not appropriately and adequately prepared or trained for the position held.

These counts should include personnel needed by public and private agencies to provide early intervention services.

TABLE 4

REPORT OF FEDERAL, STATE, AND LOCAL FUNDS EXPENDED FOR
EARLY INTERVENTION SERVICES

1987–1988 SCHOOL YEAR

Instructions

This report is authorized under 20 U.S.C. 1418(b)(4)

Provide the amount of funds expended specifically for early intervention services
in the 1987–88 school year. Do not include costs associated with capital outlays
(buildings and construction). Place zeroes (0) in source categories for which no
funds were expended. Forms are due by November 1, 1990.

Provide the amount of funds expended during school year 1987–88 for early intervention services, by each source category (i.e., Federal, State, and local sources).
If possible, each entry should represent actual expenditures. Indicate if the expenditures provided represent actual expenditures or estimated expenditures by placing an "X" in the appropriate box. Funds expended may be based upon a sampling
of data from State agencies including State and local service agencies. When sampling is used, a description of the sampling methodology must be submitted to
OSEP for approval by September 1, 1989.

TABLE 5

REPORT OF EARLY INTERVENTION SERVICES IN NEED OF
IMPROVEMENT

(1988–1989 School Year)

Instructions

This report is authorized under 20 U.S.C. 1418(b)(6).

This form requires that States identify early intervention services in need of improvement, describe the nature of the improvement needed, and indicate the number of handicapped infants and toddlers in need of these improved services. Include a description of the personnel needed to provide these services. Improved services consist of services that are: (a) not currently available for handicapped infants and toddlers; (b) in short supply for specific populations; and (c) in a stage where considerable development is necessary for the service to have maximum effectiveness or be delivered efficiently.

States may obtain needed information to complete this form through whatever means are appropriate. States are not required to have LEAs complete this form.

Indicate three to five early intervention services in greatest need of improvement. (See, for example, services and definitions listed under Table 2.) Rank these services according to need; i.e., #1 is the highest priority need, #2 is the second highest priority need, etc.

For each service needing improvement, provide a brief narrative description of the nature of improvement(s) needed. In this narrative, include the number of handicapped infants and toddlers in need of improved services and the number and type of personnel needed to provide these services. If more space is needed, please attach additional pages.

Forms are due by November 1, 1989.

TABLE 1

U.S. DEPARTMENT OF EDUCATION
OFFICE OF SPECIAL EDUCATION
AND REHABILITATIVE SERVICES
OFFICE OF SPECIAL EDUCATION
PROGRAMS

**REPORT OF HANDICAPPED INFANTS AND TODDLERS RECEIVING
EARLY INTERVENTION SERVICES**
(Parts B and H, Education of the Handicapped Act)

School Year 1987–1988

OMB No. ___1820-0557___
Form Expires ___7/31/89___

STATE:

SECTION A

COUNT DATE:	MONTH	DAY	YEAR

SECTION B

NUMBER OF INFANTS AND TODDLERS RECEIVING EARLY INTERVENTION SERVICES

	0 to 1	1 to 2	2 to 3	Total
AGE AS OF DECEMBER 1, 1987				
ALL HANDICAPPING CONDITIONS				

SECTION C

NUMBER OF INFANTS AND TODDLERS IN NEED OF EARLY INTERVENTION SERVICES

	0 through 2
AGE AS OF DECEMBER 1, 1987	
ALL HANDICAPPING CONDITIONS	

TABLE 2

U.S. DEPARTMENT OF EDUCATION
OFFICE OF SPECIAL EDUCATION
AND REHABILITATIVE SERVICES
OFFICE OF SPECIAL EDUCATION
PROGRAMS

**REPORT OF EARLY INTERVENTION SERVICES PROVIDED TO
HANDICAPPED INFANTS, TODDLERS, AND THEIR FAMILIES**

1988-1989 SCHOOL YEAR

OMB No. _____ 1820-0557
Form Expires _____ 7/31/89

STATE: _____

EARLY INTERVENTION SERVICES	NUMBER OF CHILDREN 0 THROUGH 2 RECEIVING SERVICES
PSYCHOLOGICAL SERVICES (1)	
FAMILY TRAINING, COUNSELING, AND HOME VISITS (2)	
OCCUPATIONAL THERAPY (3)	
SPEECH-LANGUAGE PATHOLOGY SERVICES (4)	
AUDIOLOGICAL SERVICES (5)	
SPECIAL INSTRUCTION (6)	
PHYSICAL THERAPY (7)	
MEDICAL SERVICES (8)	
HEALTH SERVICES (9)	
OTHER EARLY INTERVENTION SERVICES (10)	
TOTAL NUMBER OF SERVICES, Rows 1-10 (11)	

TABLE 3

U.S. DEPARTMENT OF EDUCATION
OFFICE OF SPECIAL EDUCATION
AND REHABILITATIVE SERVICES
OFFICE OF SPECIAL EDUCATION
PROGRAMS

NUMBER AND TYPE OF PERSONNEL (In Full-Time Equivalency of Assignment) EMPLOYED AND ADDITIONAL PERSONNEL NEEDED TO PROVIDE EARLY INTERVENTION SERVICES FOR HANDICAPPED INFANTS AND TODDLERS IN THE 1988–1989 SCHOOL YEAR

OMB No. _____ 1820-0556

Form Expires _____ 7/31/89

STATE: _____

EARLY INTERVENTION SERVICES PERSONNEL	for ages:	(A) FTE EMPLOYED (0 through 2)	(B) FTE NEEDED (0 through 2)
SPECIAL EDUCATORS (1)			
SPEECH AND LANGUAGE PATHOLOGISTS (2)			
AUDIOLOGISTS (3)			
OCCUPATIONAL THERAPISTS (4)			
PHYSICAL THERAPISTS (5)			
PSYCHOLOGISTS (6)			
SOCIAL WORKERS (7)			
NURSES (8)			
NUTRITIONISTS (9)			
OTHER PROFESSIONAL STAFF (10)			
TOTAL, Rows 1-10 (11)			

OMB No. _____ 182-0558

Form Expires _____ 7/31/89

TABLE 4

U.S. DEPARTMENT OF EDUCATION
OFFICE OF SPECIAL EDUCATION
AND REHABILITATIVE SERVICES
OFFICE OF SPECIAL EDUCATION
PROGRAMS

REPORT OF FEDERAL, STATE, AND LOCAL FUNDS EXPENDED FOR EARLY INTERVENTION SERVICES

School Year 1987–1988

STATE: _____

SOURCE	FUNDS EXPENDED FOR EARLY INTERVENTION SERVICES (0 through 2)
Federal	
State	
Local	

U.S. DEPARTMENT OF EDUCATION
OFFICE OF SPECIAL EDUCATION
AND REHABILITATIVE SERVICES
OFFICE OF SPECIAL EDUCATION
PROGRAMS

OMB No. _____ 1820-0555
Form Expires _____ 7/31/89

TABLE 5

REPORT OF EARLY INTERVENTION SERVICES IN NEED OF IMPROVEMENT

1988–1989 SCHOOL YEAR

STATE: _____

EARLY INTERVENTION SERVICE	DESCRIPTION OF IMPROVEMENT(S) NEEDED

Note: Indicate three to five early intervention services in greatest need of improvement. For each early intervention service, provide a brief description of improvement(s) needed. In each description, include the number of handicapped infants and toddlers in need of improved services and the number and type of personnel needed to provide these services.